HAMLYN

WHO'S WHO

IN

SNOOKER

C000265352

HAMLYN

WHO'S WHO
IN
SNOOKER

IAN MORRISON

Photography by David Muscroft
and Trevor Smith

HAMLYN

Photographic acknowledgements
All photographs supplied by David Muscroft Productions

Published by
The Hamlyn Publishing Group Limited
a division of The Octopus Group plc
Michelin House, 81 Fulham Road
London SW3 6RB
and distributed for them by
Octopus Distribution Services Limited
Rushden, Northamptonshire NN10 9RZ

Copyright © The Hamlyn Publishing Group Limited 1988

All rights reserved. No part of this publication may be
reproduced, stored in a retrieval system, or transmitted in
any form or by any means, electronic, mechanical, photocopying,
recording or otherwise, without the permission of the
copyright holder and the publisher.

First published in 1988

ISBN 0 600 55713 8

Printed by Mandarin Offset, Hong Kong

CONTENTS

Introduction 7
Roger Bales 9
Mark Bennett 10
Paddy Browne 11
John Campbell 12
Robert Chaperon 13
Eddie Charlton, AM 14
Martin Clark 16
Graham Cripsey 17
Fred Davis, OBE 18
Steve Davis, MBE 20
Les Dodd 24
Tony Drago 25
Steve Duggan 26
Ray Edmonds 27
Allison Fisher 28
Neal Foulds 29
Danny Fowler 32
Peter Francisco 33
Silvino Francisco 34
Len Ganley 36
Marcel Gauvreau 36
Dave Gilbert 37
Nigel Gilbert 38
Terry Griffiths 39
Mike Hallett 43
Barry Hearn 45
Stephen Hendry 46
Alex Higgins 50
Eugene Hughes 54
Steve James 55
Joe Johnson 56
Tony Jones 58
Wayne Jones 59
Warren King 60
Tony Knowles 61
Howard Kruger 65
Steve Longworth 66

Ted Lowe 67
Jack McLaughlin 68
Murdo McLeod 69
Dave Martin 70
Tony Meo 71
Graham Miles 73
Doug Mountjoy 74
Tommy Murphy 76
Steve Newbury 77
Joe O'Boye 78
Dene O'Kane 79
Ken Owers 80
John Parrott 81
Jackie Rea 85
Ray Reardon, MBE 86
Dean Reynolds 90
David Roe 92
John Smyth 92
John Spencer 93
Kirk Stevens 97
John Street 100
David Taylor 101
Dennis Taylor 103
Cliff Thorburn, CM 107
Willie Thorne 111
John Virgo 113
Bill Werbeniuk 115
Barry West 117
Jimmy White 118
John Williams 122
Rex Williams 123
Cliff Wilson 125
Robert Winsor 126
Jon Wright 127
Jim Wych 128

INTRODUCTION

Twenty years ago an author who had suggested a who's who in snooker to a publisher would have been laughed out of the offices.

In 1968 you could have counted the number of professional snooker players on one hand. There wasn't even a proper world championship; it existed only as a challenge competition. But the whole complexion of snooker changed in 1969 thanks to the BBC 'Pot Black' programme.

Colour television was making ground in Britain and BBC producers had the foresight to introduce this new programme. Snooker, with its bright colours and clean-cut image, was ideal for

Left: Steve Davis, world's number one snooker player

Below: Stephen Hendry, thought by many to be Steve Davis' successor

television. Eight men lined up for the first series: Fred Davis, Kingsley Kennerley, Gary Owen, John Pulman, Jackie Rea, Ray Reardon, John Spencer and Rex Williams. That was about the extent of professional snooker players in Britain at the time. Most of those first eight 'Pot Black' entrants are included in this volume, testiment indeed to their staying power in a game that has become littered with talented youngsters.

When 'Pot Black' started, nobody could ever have imagined how the sport would grow in a relatively short time. In 1986 snooker was the most televised sport, ahead of cricket, horse racing and soccer, which, despite celebrating a World Cup that year, received 132 fewer hours air space than snooker.

Television has helped turn snooker into a multi-million pound sport: sponsors are quickly attrac-

ted to the game and snooker players have become household names.

Ray Reardon and John Spencer were the first men to benefit from the success of 'Pot Black'. They were sought after for exhibitions and holiday camps employed them during the summer months to entertain holidaymakers with exhibition matches. David Taylor and Graham Miles both became household names and instantly recognisable, because of their 'Pot Black' appearances.

Another turning point in the game's history came in 1977 when promoter Mike Watterson took the world championship, which had by then reverted to a knockout competition to the Crucible Theatre in Sheffield. The Crucible is now snooker's equivalent of Wembley Stadium and, like the FA Cup final, it heralds the end of

a nine-month season. The amount of television coverage of the Embassy World Championship soon increased and every match at the championship is now covered by BBC cameras.

Since the first championship moved to Sheffield many other great names have emerged. Alex Higgins and John Virgo, who were both on the scene in the pre-Crucible days, increased in popularity as entertainers and good snooker players.

Just as Muhammad Ali came along in boxing, Pele in football and Lester Piggott in horse racing, snooker saw the arrival of its own brand of extra special player when the ginger-haired youngster Steve Davis won the Coral UK Championship at Preston in 1980. But snooker had had its first 'superstar' in between the two world wars when Joe Davis added a new element of skill to the game. Now was the coming of the second great player who, despite the surname, was no relation to Joe.

Davis has totally dominated the world of professional snooker since then, despite the challenges of many leading youngsters such as Jimmy White, Neal Foulds, John Parrott and Stephen Hendry. He has also fought off any challenge to his supremacy by some of the older hands like Higgins, Cliff Thorburn, Terry Griffiths and Dennis Taylor.

Davis and his shrewd manager Barry Hearn have helped promote the game, both on and off the table, playing a major part in snooker's increasing popularity. For Hearn and his Matchroom team have taken the game to the Far East and South America as they aim to take snooker to all points of the globe.

Despite its extensive television coverage and the considerable criticism it has received over the years, snooker remains as popular as ever and more and more youngsters are taking up the sport. The quality of young players, some not even in their teens, is exceptional, with players such as Stephen Hendry capable of compiling a century when in short trousers!

All sports like to see new faces emerging and snooker is no exception with a constant flow of talented players appearing in the professional ranks. The 1987-88 season was an outstanding one for the young Scot Stephen Hendry and Liverpool's John Parrott has threatened more than once to overcome that barrier and win his first major tournament. Martin Clark has come through as a potential winner in the not too distant future while David Roe and Steve James are both capable of causing major upsets. It is also nice to see players like Steve Newbury, Mike Hallett and Dean Reynolds all get the rewards of hard work.

Compiling a who's who in any sport is never an easy job. In snooker, however, I was a little bit more fortunate. There are only 130 tournament professionals, but who do you leave out?

As a guideline the top 64 ranked players were used as a starting point. In addition men such as Fred Davis are included. His contribution to the sport has been immense and he is still playing in major tournaments.

But snooker is not only about the players who compile those big breaks on the table; there are others who have an influence on the game and they, too, have been included. There are the leading referees, without whom the quality of the matches would not be what it is. Then, of course, there are the people who have a big influence on the game these days: the managers. They are now a vital part of this multi-million pound sport.

I have also included the 'voice of snooker', Ted Lowe. Having spent a lifetime in the sport and being responsible for assembling the line-up for the inaugural 'Pot Black' in 1969, Ted is constantly being asked who is the greatest player, Steve Davis or Joe Davis. Being one of the men to have watched both Steve and Joe professionally he is perhaps the most suitably qualified person to answer such a question. His answer: 'Joe'.

The snooker season begins in one calendar year and finishes in the next (from September to May normally).

The following events are played between September and December:
   Langs Scottish Masters
   Fidelity Unit Trusts International (formerly Jameson International)
   Goya International
   BCE International
   Rothmans Grand Prix (formerly Professional Players Tournament)
   Tennents UK Open (formerly Super Crystalate UK Championship)
   Coral UK Championship, Coral UK Open
   Fosters World Doubles (formerly Hofmeister World Doubles)
The following events are played between January and May:
   Mercantile Credit Classic (formerly Wilson's Classic, Lada Classic)
   Benson & Hedges Masters
   English Professional Championship
   MIM Britannia British Open (formerly Dulux British Open)
   *Tuborg World Cup (formerly State Express World Team Classic
   Guinness World Cup, Car Care Plan World Cup)
   Benson & Hedges Irish Masters
   Embassy World Professional Championship
*From 1979-83 it was played in the first half of the season.

The rankings for each player are his ranking positions in the six seasons 1983 to 1988 inclusive. If a dash appears by any year it means the player was a professional but had not scored any points towards the official ranking list.
The number of players ranked over those seasons were:
1983 32; 1984 61; 1985 102; 1986 118; 1987 130; 1988 133

Ian Morrison 1988

ROGER BALES

Born: 15 August 1948, Birmingham, England

Turned professional 1984

First ranking points: 1986 Dulux British Open

When Roger Bales received his letter saying he had been accepted as a member of the World Professional Billiards and Snooker Association (WPBSA) he described it as the 'greatest thrill of his life'. The clean-cut evening-dress image of the professional snooker player was no problem to Roger, because he was used to wearing a dinner jacket. He was working as a Birmingham casino manager at the time.

Born and bred in Birmingham, he had a brief spell away from his beloved city in the early 1980s when he worked in Manchester but he later returned to his home town.

It was in Birmingham, at the Burton Snooker Hall in Selly Oak, that Roger first started playing snooker at the age of 13. As an amateur his first notable achievement was in winning the National Pairs title with Clive Everton in 1977. After winning the Pontins Autumn Open in 1983 he realised he could compete against the best players and the following year he applied for professional status.

Eight wins but no ranking points

In his first year as a pro he won eight matches yet surprisingly did not pick up a ranking point. He finished the season ranked 100 and improved 34 places the next season when, towards the end of the season, he collected his first point thanks to a magnificent win over world champion Dennis Taylor in the third round of the Dulux British Open.

He led Taylor 3-0 and 4-2 before being pulled back to 4-4. He then produced a 61 break to win the match. Rex Williams, whom Roger practises with a lot, beat him in the next round but Bales had, at last, proved himself.

Convinced he could improve after that win, Roger gave up his casino job and spent all summer practising for the new season. At 8 am he could be seen on the table at the Astra Snooker Club.

He made another slight move up the rankings in 1987 when his best result was to reach the fourth round of the BCE International with wins over Fred Davis and Kirk Stevens, his only two of the season.

CAREER HIGHLIGHTS

1977
National Pairs Champion
(with Clive Everton)

1983
Pontins Autumn Open
Champion

1986
Dulux British Open
Championship (last 32)

1987
Rothmans Grand Prix
(last 32)

Rankings

Year	Ranking
1985	100
1986	66
1987	57
1988	60

A former casino manager, Birmingham's Roger Bales now plays snooker full-time

MARK BENNETT

Born: 23 September 1963, Blackwood, Monmouthshire, Wales

Turned professional: 1986

First ranking points: 1986 Rothmans Grand Prix

CAREER HIGHLIGHTS

1985
Welsh Amateur Champion

1986
Rothmans Grand Prix
(last 32)

1987
Embassy World Professional
Championship (last 32)

1988
Mercantile Credit Classic
(last 32)

Ranking
1987   54
1988   52

Typical of many lower-ranked professionals, Welshman Mark Bennett did not book into a hotel for the duration of the qualifying competition for the 1987 Embassy World Professional Championships at Preston. He made a booking for only one night. Because he won all four of his qualifying matches he had to book into four different hotels during his stay in the north-west. He crowned a memorable debut season by beating Bill Werbenuik 10-8 and reaching the Crucible at the first attempt.

The latest in the long line of great players to come from Wales, Bennett distinguished himself in 1985 when he added his name to the impressive list of winners of the Welsh Amateur. That win made Mark eligible for the World Amateur Championship at Blackpool and after winning all 11 of his group matches he was the favourite to capture the title but then lost to team-mate Dilwyn John, a former Cardiff City goalkeeper, in the quarter-final. Bennett had beaten John to win the Welsh title a few months earlier.

First pro application rejected

Earlier in 1985 Mark had applied for professional status, but this was rejected. However, the new pro-ticket series gave him a chance to get into the paid ranks and he duly qualified before taking up his professional status in 1986.

An attacking player and a fluent potter, he had a good first year as a professional winning 11 of his 18 matches, his biggest win being his 10-8 victory over Werbeniuk after trailing 7-4. His opponent in the next round was Dennis Taylor and the former champion ran out the 10-4 winner.

Straight after the match Howard Kruger, Alex Higgins' manager, signed Bennett for the Framework team, although Bennett's long-standing manager Chris Bunn continued in that capacity.

Mark Bennett like Reardon, Wilson, Mountjoy and Griffiths, a Welsh Amateur champion who joined the professional game

PADDY BROWNE

Born: 1 March 1965, Dublin, Republic of Ireland

Turned professional: 1983

First ranking points: 1986 Mercantile Credit Classic

CAREER HIGHLIGHTS

1982
Republic of Ireland Amateur Champion

1986
Rothmans Grand Prix (last 16)

Rankings

Year	Ranking
1985	61
1986	48
1987	43
1988	54

'Who knows Paddy Browne?' asked the Granada Television programme 'Northern Echoes' in 1985 during a documentary about the life of a struggling professional snooker player.

Paddy was seen having to make his way to snooker matches on the bus, a far cry from the chauffeur-driven superstars of the game. One who really did know Paddy Browne was his wife Susan, who has stood behind Paddy in his quest for stardom.

Snooker's youngest professional

Born in Dublin but now living in Manchester, where he was brought up in the tough world of money-match snooker, Paddy became the youngest Republic of Ireland amateur champion in 1982 when only 17 years of age. The following year he became the game's young-est professional (a distinction since held by Stephen Hendry).

Granada Television gave a realistic assessment of the life of Paddy Browne. It has been a struggle, but thankfully some of the worry was taken from him when he joined the Robert Winsor stable in 1987. That move was because of Susan. She wrote to Winsor stating that she felt her husband needed the security of a professional organisation like Robert Winsor International behind him. Winsor was impressed with Susan's letter and invited the pair of them to his palatial home in north London and that was that. Paddy Browne joined the team and had the security of proper management behind him.

Paddy struggled to get beyond qualifying rounds in his early days as a professional but in the 1986 Rothmans Grand Prix he enjoyed his best success to date when he reached the last 16 before losing to Stephen Hendry. On the way he beat world champion Joe Johnson 5-2.

He struggled at the start of the 1987-88 season but picked up a welcome ranking point in the MIM Britannia British Open.

Paddy Browne, the youngest-ever winner of the Irish amateur title, which he won at the age of 17 in 1982

JOHN CAMPBELL

Born: 10 April 1953, Brisbane, Queensland, Australia

Turned professional: 1982

First ranking points: 1983 Professional Players Tournament

CAREER HIGHLIGHTS

1979
Australian Amateur Champion

1983
Professional Players
Tournament (quarter-final)

1985
Australian Professional
Champion
Winfield Australian Masters
(runner-up)

1986
Embassy World Professional
Championship (last 16)

Rankings
1983	39
1984	28
1985	31
1986	18
1987	22
1988	33

Eddie Charlton had dominated the Australian Professional Championship since 1964 before John Campbell broke his monopoly by beating Australia's number one 10-7 in the 1985 final. Now, Campbell and his contemporary Warren King are challenging Charlton for supremacy in their home country.

The 6 ft 4 in (1.9 m) Campbell left school at 15 and went to work in a biscuit factory. He started playing pool and snooker at 16 at the Brisbane West End club, and at 21 was the Queensland State snooker champion. He became too good for the locals and had to move to Sydney for better opposition. That was when he first met Warren King. In 1979 he took the Australian amateur title and beat Eddie Charlton for the first time at the City Tatts in Sydney. Three years later he turned professional.

Makes his home in England

Campbell's first professional event in England was the 1983 Embassy and he reached the Crucible stage at the first attempt, but lost 10-5 to Cliff Thorburn. John stayed in Britain and lived with some friends in Sheffield before moving to London. But after meeting Willie Thorne he moved to Leicester and played most of his snooker at Willie's club, and it was there that he made his first-ever maximum.

In the Professional Players Tournament at the start of the 1983-84 season John beat the three 'Ms' – Mountjoy, Miles and Martin – to book a quarter-final meeting with Tony Knowles, but the Lancashire player ran out the 5-3 victor. Having missed out on qualifying for the Crucible in 1984 John made it in 1985 and his television appearance was the first of three great matches with Eddie Charlton over a three-month period.

At Sheffield the master had the initiative with a comfortable 10-3 win but in the Winfield Masters John gained revenge by winning their quarter-final match 5-4. In the semi-final, Campbell had the best win of his career in beating John Parrott 6-4. Tony Meo, however, was too good for him in the final, and won 7-2. But in the next tournament Campbell beat Robby Foldvari and Warren King to line up for the third time against Charlton in the final of the Australian Professional Championship.

Campbell ends Charlton's long reign

Apart from a hiccup in 1968, Charlton had held the title continuously since 1964 but John opened a new chapter in Australian

John Campbell, the man who ended Eddie Charlton's long reign as top Australian snooker player

snooker history by beating him 10-7. While in Australia a friend, who is a rugby league coach, loaned John a book entitled the *Psychology of Winning* and that, together with his own abundant talent, helped improve his game.

He teamed up with fellow Australasian Dene O'Kane under Peter Herod's management, got the resident professional's job at the Connaught Club in London, and moved into his own flat. Everything was ideal, and the settled atmosphere showed in John's play in 1985-86 as he picked up a total of 11 ranking points, including at least one in every ranking event, to finish just outside the top 16 in 18th place, the highest placed Australian. He also won his first match at the Crucible when he beat Ray Reardon 10-8 in the first round to become the first person ever to beat Reardon at that stage of the competition. Campbell lost to his friend Thorne at the next stage.

John helped Australia to reach the final of the Fersina World Cup in 1988, their best ever performance.

ROBERT CHAPERON

Born: 18 May 1958, Sudbury, Ontario, Canada

Turned professional: 1983

First ranking points: 1985 Dulux British Open

CAREER HIGHLIGHTS

1981
Canadian Amateur Snooker Champion
Canadian Amateur Billiards Champion

1982
Canadian Amateur Billiards Champion

1985
Canadian Professional Championship (runner-up)

1987
Rothmans Grand Prix (quarter-final)

Rankings
1985	44
1986	53
1987	41
1988	29

Robert Chaperon was brought up in the world of money-matches before turning professional in 1983. A dual billiards and snooker champion in his homeland, Robert first came to Britain in 1983, with £50. However, he won £1,000 in his first tournament. He enjoyed a good run in the 1984–85 Dulux British Open, where he had wins over Patsy Fagan, fellow-Canadian Bill Werbeniuk, and Wayne Jones before losing to Silvino Francisco in the third round. A narrow 10-9 defeat by the former champion Fred Davis in the World Championship deprived Robert of a chance to appear at the Crucible at his first attempt.

Canada's number two player

A move to the Gainsborough Snooker Centre, where he became the resident professional in 1985, gave Robert's game a lift and that summer he reached the final of the Canadian Professional Championship. A fine 6-4 win over Kirk Stevens in the quarter-final and a 6-3 win over Frank Jonik in the semi-final pitched Robert against Cliff Thorburn, the man who inspired his career. Former champion Thorburn was just that little bit too good for Chaperon on the day and Cliff won 6-4. Back in Britain Chaperon's best result of the season was a revenge win over Silvino Francisco in the Goya but there was little else for him to enjoy about the season and he dropped nine ranking places.

However, the 1986-87 season was a different story and he enjoyed his best season on the professional circuit. He collected three ranking points and won just over £10,000 in prize-money. A large part of his success was due to reaching the fifth round of the BCE International at Stoke-on-Trent, where he enjoyed fine wins over Dave Martin and Tony Drago before Eugene Hughes put him out 5-0. In the next tournament, the Rothmans Grand Prix, Robert beat former world champion Ray Reardon, but then had virtually no more success that season.

His pattern of starting a season well continued in 1987-88 when he reached the televised stage of the Fidelity Unit Trusts International but John Parrott put paid to any further quest for glory Chaperon had by winning 5-1.

After a slow start on the professional circuit Robert has reached the top 32 by reaching the quarter-final of the 1987 Rothmans Grand Prix and he reached the Crucible stage of the World Championship in 1988.

Canadian Robert Chaperon is now starting to show his true ability and is proving to be a tough player to beat

EDDIE CHARLTON, AM

Born: 31 October 1929, Merewether, New South Wales, Australia

Turned professional: 1963

First ranking points: 1974 World Professional Championship

In Walter and Horace Lindrum Australia has produced two of the greatest names in billiards and snooker. Eddie Charlton had quite a task on his hands in living up to the high reputation of those two, but he has done it, and with great pride. Although Charlton has never won the World Championship, either at billiards or snooker, he has been a great ambassador for his country and a much respected professional for 25 years.

All-round sportsman

Born in Merewether in New South Wales, Charlton was brought up in nearby Swansea along with brother Jim, who is also a professional snooker player in Australia. Eddie was an all-round sportsman as a youngster and was a senior grade footballer for ten years. He was also a member of the Swansea Belmont crew that won the Australian surfing championship. Cricket, roller-skating, athletics and boxing were among Eddie's other loves. But his proudest sporting moment came in 1956 when he and Jim carried the Olympic torch part of the way on its journey to the Melbourne Olympic Games.

A former coalminer, Charlton and his colleagues once staged a five-day strike underground . . . to pass away their time they arranged for a table-tennis table and dartboard to be lowered underground. Charlton found two more sports that he was quite good at!

Eddie was 34 when he turned professional, and in 1964 he became the Australian Professional Champion, a title he was to hold until beaten by John Campbell in 1984. Only defeat by Warren Simpson in 1968 prevented an uninterrupted 20-year reign.

He first made the trip to England in 1968 to challenge John Pulman for the World Snooker Championship at Bolton, but he returned without the title after the Englishman successfully defended with a 39-34 win. The following year the Championship reverted to a knock-out competition and in November 1970 Eddie helped in the organisation of the Championship in Australia. That was his first appearance in the new style of competition, and he has competed in every Championship since, but the title has eluded him.

Two finals, two defeats . . . but still a world champion

He has appeared in two finals, and lost to Ray Reardon each time. The first was at the Manchester City Exhibition Hall in 1973 and the second in 1975 when Reardon

---

'The reason I haven't won the World Championship is because I wasn't good enough.'

An honest confession from Eddie

---

won by one frame, 31-30, at the Nunawading Basketball Centre, Melbourne, when Charlton again helped with the promotion and organisation.

Although he has never won the World Championship Eddie proudly boasts to be a reigning world champion . . . the world match-play champion. The event, promoted by Charlton, was staged at Melbourne in 1976 and given the approval of the WPBSA, who accorded it 'world' status. Charlton beat Reardon 31-24 and, as the Championship has not been held since, can justly claim to be the reigning world match-play champion.

Eddie has done a lot to promote and develop the game in his home country and was instrumental in the formation of the Australian Professional Players Association. He played a large part in getting the leading professionals like Reardon and John Spencer to tour his country in the 1970s. And the famous Eddie Charlton Circus was a popular touring event in Australia when Eddie, son Edward and Eddie's brother Jim would take the game of snooker to parts of the

Eddie Charlton, the man who dominated Australian billiards and snooker for twenty years. There is no doubting the influence he had on other younger players in his home country who tried to emulate him

CAREER HIGHLIGHTS

1964-67
Australian Professional
Champion

1968
World Professional
Championship (runner-up)

1969-84
Australian Professional
Champion

1972
'Pot Black' Champion

1973
World Professional
Championship (runner-up)
'Pot Black' Champion

1975
World Professional
Championship (runner-up)

1976
World Match-Play Champion

1980
'Pot Black' Champion

Rankings

1983	6
1984	6
1985	12
1986	25
1987	26
1988	19

country that would otherwise be starved of seeing such talented players. For his services to billiards and snooker Eddie was awarded the Australian Order of Merit in 1980.

It is not only at snooker that Eddie has made his name. Three times he has come close to winning the World Billiards Championship. He lost to Rex Williams in 1974 and 1976, and to Mark Wildman in 1984.

Tough competitor

Charlton did not start playing snooker regularly on the British circuit until the early 1980s, but with the introduction of further ranking tournaments (at one time the World Championship was the

Concentration has been one of Eddie Charlton's biggest assets and make him a hard man to beat. It is little wonder he is nicknamed 'steady Eddie'

only ranking event) he started playing more often to try to maintain his high position – he was ranked number three every year from 1976 to 1980. But he has yet to win a ranking event, his best result being in the 1983 Jameson

---

Alex Higgins once said of Charlton:

'We don't get on. In fact I don't like him. But sometimes I wish I could be like him.'

International when he reached the semi-final before losing 9-2 to Steve Davis. In 1988 he was in the Australian team which reached the Fersina World Cup final.

A very tough competitor, Eddie is hard to beat and does not accept defeat until the last black is potted. He spends less time competing in England these days, and more time in Australia helping to develop the game, but all professionals know that if they draw Eddie they are in for a tough match. His supremacy as Australia's top player has been challenged in recent years by John Campbell and Warren King but Eddie Charlton will remain a billiards and snooker legend in Australia, just as Walter and Horace Lindrum were before him.

MARTIN CLARK

Born: 27 October 1968, Wolverhampton, Staffordshire, England

Turned professional: 1987

First ranking points: 1987 Fidelity Unit Trusts International

CAREER HIGHLIGHTS

1984
National Under-19 Champion

1987
Fidelity Unit Trusts
International (last 16)

1988
Mercantile Credit Classic
(last 16)

Ranking
1988   41

Martin Clark caused quite a stir in his first seven matches as a professional in 1987 when he beat, among others, Neal Foulds and Dennis Taylor. But the youngster from the West Midlands has been raising eyebrows since 1984. It was in that year that he became the youngest winner of the British Under-19 Championship at the age of 15. And two years later in the Home International series at Heysham he compiled a break of 141 which was later ratified as a new record break by a non-professional, superseding the 140 made by Joe Johnson in 1978.

£26,000 winnings as an 'amateur'

The professional ticket series gave Martin the chance to gain professional status, but in his final season as an 'amateur' he won more than £26,000.

Early professional success saw him reach the televised stage of the Fidelity Unit Trusts International

at Trentham Gardens where he handed former world champion Dennis Taylor a 5-0 whitewash, which Taylor described as 'The best television debut any player has ever had.' Irishman Joe O'Boye ended Clark's run in the next round but Martin had arrived as the latest wonder boy of snooker. He is a brilliant long potter and breakbuilder. Alex Higgins' manager Howard Kruger saw Martin's potential and recruited him as a member of his Framework team.

In his highly successful debut season he collected further ranking points in the Tennents and Mercantile. His greatest moment was in the World Doubles: with Jimmy Chambers he beat the holders Steve Davis and Tony Meo as 250-1 outsiders.

Martin started playing snooker at the age of 13, and made a 57 break on his first visit to the table. Graham Morris, proprietor of the Dudley Snooker Centre, managed him from the age of 14.

In 1988 he reached the final of the Kent Cup in Peking, losing to John Parrott before over 100 million Chinese televiewers.

The youngster tipped as a future world champion, Martin Clark from Sedgeley

GRAHAM CRIPSEY

Born: 8 December 1954, Skegness, Lincolnshire, England

Turned professional: 1982

First ranking points: 1985 Coral UK Open

CAREER HIGHLIGHTS

1980
WMC & IU Snooker
Champion

1987
Rothmans Grand Prix
(last 16)

Rankings
1983	—
1984	—
1985	89
1986	50
1987	48
1988	46

He has part of his left thumb missing; he looks like a bank manager; and he used to be a wall of death rider . . . yet despite all that, Graham Cripsey is a very good snooker player.

For 14 years Graham, his brother Gary and their parents owned a wall of death business at Skegness. Graham was 15 when he joined the business (two years after he first started playing snooker at Henry Smith's club in Skegness). In all his time on the wall he fell off only five times, but one of the accidents led to him losing part of his left thumb. Fortunately, it did not affect his snooker.

From wall of death to snooker professional in two years

Graham soon realised he was a good snooker player, but did not at first consider turning professional. He won the prestigious Working Men's Club and Institute Union Snooker Championship for the Skegness WMC in 1980, but only after the family sold the business in 1982 did Graham decide to concentrate on his snooker and try and get into the professional ranks. He was accepted as a professional that year but it was not until the 1985 English Professional Championship that he progressed beyond the qualifying stage of any competition. That signalled the start of Graham's rise up the rankings. He picked up ranking points in the following season's Mercantile Credit Classic and Coral UK Open, with creditable wins over Cliff Wilson, Steve Newbury and John Spencer.

In an effort to improve his game, Graham and wife Carol moved to London in 1986 to enable Graham to get practice against better players (he has always been a believer in not taking on players he can beat easily. Doing so, he thinks, might be good for his morale, but not good for his game). He took a job as resident professional at Rowans, in Finsbury Park. Carol has supported Graham tremendously in his snooker career and she even sold her Skegness boutique in order to move to London with him.

He collected another ranking point in the 1987 Dulux and started the 1987–88 season by reaching the last 16 of a ranking tournament for the first time in his career when he got to the fifth round of the Rothmans Grand Prix at Reading before losing to Peter Francisco.

Former wall-of-death rider turned snooker player, Graham Cripsey

'There IS life beyond Skegness!'

Graham's reaction after leaving Skegness and moving to London

'I love playing snooker but it's harder than the wall of death . . .

Self-explanatory comments from Graham

FRED DAVIS, OBE

Born: 14 August 1913, Whittingham Moor, Derbyshire, England

Turned professional: 1929

First ranking points: 1974 World Professional Snooker Championship

Fred Davis' ranking positions may show a decline in recent years but when you consider his age that is hardly surprising. He is still a frequent participant in the ranking events in his mid-70s, more than 50 years after turning professional, and he still has the same infectious love of both billiards and snooker.

The younger half of the famous Davis brothers that dominated snooker for 30 years, Fred was 12 years younger than Joe and, because of the age gap, they shared little of their childhood. But Joe's success on the billiard table spurred Fred to follow him, and in 1929 Fred was the National Under-16 Billiards Champion. He turned professional shortly afterwards and soon made an impression by winning the junior professional title three years in succession.

Out of Joe's shadow

Having lived in Joe's shadow for a long time Fred was anxious to do well in his first World Championship in 1937, but Welshman Bill Withers had other ideas. Joe, however, restored the Davis family pride by beating Withers 30-1 in the next round.

Fred and Joe met many times but only once in the World Championship final. But what a treat they dished up to the fans at Thurston's Hall in 1940 when Joe won by the narrowest of margins, 37-36.

When Joe retired from world championship play after winning the 1946 world crown it was the ideal opportunity for Fred to succeed him but the Scot Walter Donaldson beat Fred in the 1947 final. Fred went on to capture the title a year later and he retained it in

Snooker's 'Grand Old Man' Fred Davis, no longer a winner, but as popular as ever

1949, beating Donaldson both times. Donaldson regained the title in 1950 but Fred recaptured it the following year. Between 1952 and 1956 Fred was the winner of the Professional Match-Play title which was the world championship in all but name.

As the game went into a depression in the 1950s Fred carried on playing exhibition matches, and ran a hotel in Llandudno, North Wales. He suffered a heart attack in 1970, and a second one in 1974 but he recovered to reach the semi-final of the World Championship that year, only to lose to Ray Reardon. In 1979 Fred was honoured with the captaincy of the England team in the inaugural World Cup competition and led them to second place behind Wales.

World champion at 67

Despite his many great moments in the sport the one title that had eluded Fred was the World Profes-

sional Billiards Championship. A lover of the three-ball game, that omission was repaired in May 1980 when he beat Rex Williams for the title, to become only the second man after his brother Joe to hold both billiards and snooker world championships. Fred was 66 at the time of the win, and he retained the title six months later.

In recent years Fred has struggled against the new young up-and-coming snooker players, but in 1985-86 he arrested his slide

---

When his delayed world championship match with Dean Reynolds in 1982 had to be continued between the morning and afternoon sessions in front of a deserted hall

'This is more like it used to be in the old days.'

CAREER HIGHLIGHTS

1929
National Under-16 Billiards Champion

1948-49
World Professional Snooker Champion

1951
World Professional Snooker Champion
United Kingdom Professional Billiards Champion

1952-56
Professional Match-Play Snooker Champion

1958-59
News of the World *Snooker Champion*

1980
World Professional Billiards Champion (twice)

Rankings

Year	Ranking
1983	28
1984	46
1985	56
1986	47
1987	61
1988	83

'Promise me not to retire until I've beaten you.'

That was the request of Kirk Stevens to Fred after Davis had beaten the Canadian in the 1986 Mercantile. It was the third time in three meetings Fred had won

down the rankings and actually moved up nine places, thanks to wins over Bill Werbeniuk and another Canadian, Kirk Stevens,

'The day I need anything to make me play snooker is the day I give up.'

Fred talking in 1987 about the Beta Blocker stories that constantly hit the headlines

that earned Fred ranking points in the Coral UK Open and Mercantile Credit Classic.

Fred is delighted with the rebirth of snooker. He may not be winning any more but there is not a more popular character on the circuit than the sport's 'Grand Old Man'. For his services to snooker Fred was awarded the OBE in 1977.

Fred Davies, still going strong, a man who has seen many changes in snooker.

The following year his famous brother died, shortly after watching Fred's epic world championship semi-final encounter with South Africa's Perrie Mans.

The game's senior citizen

Fred Davis is by eight years the game's oldest current professional playing member of the WPBSA.

		Year born
1	FRED DAVIS	1913
2	Jack Rea	1921
3	John Dunning	1927
4	Jack Fitzmaurice	1928
5	George Scott	1929
6	Eddie Charlton	1929
7	Pat Houlihan	1929

STEVE DAVIS, MBE

Born: 22 August 1957, Plumstead, London, England

Turned professional: 1978

First ranking points: 1979 Embassy World Professional Championship

As you would expect, Steve is just as competitive at other sports, notably golf. He is seen here with Nick Faldo, the 1987 British Open golf champion

Steve Davis has those qualities rarely found in true British professional sportsmen: dedication, the insatiable appetite for winning and the hatred of not winning. That last quality was at its most obvious at the end of that epic World Championship final at the Crucible in 1985 when Dennis Taylor beat Davis on the last black. BBC interviewer David Vine asked Davis how he felt immediately after the match. 'Great. It's really great to lose,' said Steve with more than a touch of sarcasm in his voice. For a man used to nothing but success, failure is hard.

Davis first played snooker when he was 12. The family were on holiday at a Pontins camp and Steve's father, 'Gunboat' Bill, no mean player himself, took Steve for a game. The youngster took to it instantly and when they returned home he continued playing with his dad at the Plumstead Labour Club. Mother Jean was not too keen on her son playing so much snooker. Steve obtained five GCE O-level passes and when he started A-level studies his mum saw a bright future for Steve in something like banking or accountancy. But snooker gradually took over his life, and his studies were abandoned at 17 in order to play billiards and snooker full-time. To supplement his pocket money he worked as a delivery boy for a greengrocer and then a butcher.

The start of the Davis–Hearn relationship

The 'career' of Steve Davis started in 1976 when he beat Ian Williamson to win the Under-19 Billiards Championship. Steve used to play at the Romford branch of the Luc-

> **'Winning this is better than 1981 because I've experienced the trauma of getting beaten in the final and it's horrible.'**
>
> *Steve after winning back the world title in 1987*

ania snooker empire and the talent of this youngster was brought to the notice of Barry Hearn by Vic Harris. Hearn, a shrewd businessman, had a contract drawn up and so was born one of the best relationships in sport. It spreads further than manager and superstar because they are the best of friends.

Davis ended his amateur career with international honours and by winning the prestigious WMC & IU snooker title. He also reached the billiards final but lost to the more experienced Norman Dagley. One of his last wins as an amateur was in beating his current stablemate Tony Meo in the final to win the Pontins Open Championship.

Davis turned professional in September 1978 and at the end of the season he reached the first round proper of the World Championship but lost 13-11 to Dennis Taylor, who went on to lose to Terry Griffiths in the final.

If Griffiths was the hero in 1979 then that honour fell to Davis a year later when he knocked out the

Steve relaxes with his father Bill (a good class club player), and the world championship trophy

defending champion at the first hurdle before losing 13-9 to Alex Higgins in the quarter-final. That was the first of the many meetings the two rivals have engaged in over the years. Steve's performance at the Crucible received rave notices from the media and his first title was predictably not too far away. In November 1980 he beat Terry Griffiths 9-0 in the semi-final of the Coral UK Championship and then went on to register his first win over Higgins by beating him 16-6 in the final. A new star was born.

Two wins in a week, then a world title

A week after pocketing the £6,000 winner's cheque Steve won another £5,000 for winning the Wilson's Classic at Bolton. In quick succession he added the Yamaha International Masters and English Professional titles before winding up a great second season by beating Welshman Doug Mountjoy 18-12 to win his first World Championship.

The winning carried on into the

CAREER HIGHLIGHTS

1976
National Under-19 Billiards Champion

1978
WMC & IU Snooker Champion

1980
Coral UK Champion

1981
Yamaha International Masters Champion
Courage English Professional Champion
Embassy World Professional Champion
Jameson International Champion
Coral UK Champion
State Express World Team Classic (member of winning England team)

1982
Benson & Hedges Masters Champion
Yamaha International Masters Champion
Tolly Cobbold Classic Champion
Langs Scottish Masters Champion
Hofmeister World Doubles Champion (with Tony Meo)

1983
Lada Classic Champion
Tolly Cobbold Classic Champion
Benson & Hedges Irish Masters Champion
Embassy World Professional Champion
Langs Scottish Masters Champion

Jameson International Champion
State Express World Team Classic (member of winning England team)
Hofmeister World Doubles Champion (with Tony Meo)

1984
Lada Classic Champion
Benson & Hedges Irish Masters Champion
Tolly Cobbold Classic Champion
Embassy World Professional Champion
Langs Scottish Masters Champion
Jameson International Champion
Coral UK Open Champion

1985
Tolly Cobbold English Professional Champion
Rothmans Grand Prix Champion
Coral UK Open Champion
Hofmeister World Doubles Champion (with Tony Meo)

1986
Dulux British Open Champion

Tennents United Kingdom Open Champion
Hofmeister World Doubles Champion (with Tony Meo)

1987
Mercantile Credit Classic Champion
Benson & Hedges Irish Masters Champion
Embassy World Professional Champion
Fidelity Unit Trusts International Champion
Tennents United Kingdom Open Championship

1988
Mercantile Credit Classic Champion
Benson & Hedges Masters Champion
Fersina World Cup (member of winning England team)
Benson & Hedges Irish Masters Champion
Embassy World Professional Champion

Rankings

1983	1	1986	1
1984	1	1987	1
1985	1	1988	1

His record at the Crucible

Since making his debut at the Crucible in 1979 Steve has only three times failed to reach the World Championship final. His year-by-year record is as follows:

Year	Round	Opponent	Result	Score
1979	First round	v Dennis Taylor	lost	11-13
1980	Quarter-final	v Alex Higgins	lost	9-13
1981	Final	v Doug Mountjoy	won	18-12
1982	First round	v Tony Knowles	lost	1-10
1983	Final	v Cliff Thorburn	won	18-6
1984	Final	v Jimmy White	won	18-16
1985	Final	v Dennis Taylor	lost	17-18
1986	Final	v Joe Johnson	lost	12-18
1987	Final	v Joe Johnson	won	18-14
1988	Final	v Terry Griffiths	won	18-11

The greatest snooker player of all time, Steve Davis

1981-82 season, starting with a resounding 9-0 beating of Dennis Taylor in the final of the Jameson International. Terry Griffiths was well beaten, 16-3, by Davis as he successfully defended his Coral UK Championship, and it was again Griffiths who lost to Davis in the final of the Benson & Hedges Masters and Yamaha International Masters in successive competitions.

A 10-1 shocker

When the 1982 Word Championship came around the bookmakers would not entertain any winner other than Davis. He was paired against a complete outsider, and professional of only 18 months, Lancastrian Tony Knowles. However, Knowles upset all the odds and won by a staggering 10-1 margin. It was the biggest upset the sport has ever seen.

That defeat, however, was possibly the spur Davis needed. He had started to look invincible but his defeat gave renewed hope to his fellow professionals. But they should have known better because Davis won the Scottish Masters, Lada Classic, Tolly Cobbold Classic and the Benson & Hedges Irish Masters en route to the 1983 World Championship.

Once at the Crucible, only Dennis Taylor in the second round offered any resistance to Davis' charge towards a second title. After he had beaten Alex Higgins 16-5 in the semi-final victory seemed a formality – and it was. Cliff Thorburn, drained after three successive epic matches that went on into the early hours of the morning, could offer no challenge to Davis, who regained his title with an 18-6 win.

Davis set his sights on becoming the first man to retain his title at the Crucible in 1984 and he prepared for the championship by winning most tournaments along the way. A surprise defeat by Mike Hallett in the Professional Players Tournament, a 16-15 defeat in a classic Coral UK final by Alex Higgins and a quarter-final defeat by Kirk Stevens in the Benson & Hedges Masters at Wembley were Steve's only reversals in an otherwise impeccable season. It culminated in him fulfilling his ambition and retaining his world title after a great final with Jimmy White, which Steve won 18-16.

One of snooker's great finals

If that final was a great one then twelve months later he was involved in one even greater. This time it was the likeable Irishman Dennis Taylor who provided the opposition in one of the most enthralling matches seen in modern snooker. The 35-frame final went to the very last black and the intensity of the occasion got to both players as they missed what would normally be easy shots for them, until Taylor sank the match-winning ball.

That disappointment for Davis was hard to swallow but he came back with more determination. With some blistering performances he beat Alex Higgins 5-0 in the fifth round of the Rothmans Grand Prix, Cliff Thorburn 8-1 in the Canadian Masters, Higgins 6-1 in the Kit Kat Break for Champions, and had easy wins over Doug Mountjoy and Jimmy White as he sought to regain his world crown. Davis was desperate to win

back his title, but Yorkshireman Joe Johnson had different ideas and he ran out the surprise 18-12 winner.

After two successive defeats at the Crucible Davis was left wondering what had happened to his game. He was the master at playing in the tense atmosphere of snooker's best known venue but all of a sudden he had lost two finals.

Desperate to win back the world crown

The money was no longer Steve's motivation for success as he had become the sport's first millionaire. Winning titles was his obsession and in particular he wanted the world title. In 1987 he was to get it. Apart from a nervous opening match against Australian Warren King, Steve's passage to the final was fairly comfortable. Once more he met Joe Johnson, a surprise finalist for the second successive year, and Davis had extra reason for wanting to settle the score and get his hands back on the trophy. Despite the Yorkshireman's brave effort Davis achieved his aim and won 18-14. The 'King' had at last got back his crown.

The appetite for winning was not lost in 1987–88 as Steve won three of the first four ranking tournaments of the season, won the last four frames to lead England to

'He was pacing up and down like an expectant father.'

John Parris, cue-repairer, after performing a seven-hour operation on Davis' trusty ash cue in 1987 when he had to turn it into a two-piece cue after it had split near the ferrule

'I don't believe Steve is as far out on his own as a lot of people believe and I aim to prove that point in our semi-final tomorrow.'

Jimmy White before his meeting with Steve in the 1981 Coral UK Championship . . . Davis won 9-0!

Above: The master tactician at work. Concentration and determination are part of Steve Davis' successful game

Right: Celebrating after recapturing the world title from Joe Johnson in 1987

victory in the Fersina World Cup and ended by winning his fifth World Championship.

Steve Davis is more than the best snooker player in the world, he is a great ambassador for the game. His superb manners on and off the table are a good advertisement for the sport and it is that, allied with Barry Hearn's shrewd business brain, that has helped develop snooker worldwide, particularly in Europe and in the Far East, where Davis is rapidly becoming as recognisable a figure as Muhammad Ali was in the 1960s and 1970s.

The trappings of success have been great for Steve and manager Hearn. Steve's one pride and joy is his Porsche, but that represents a small percentage of his great wealth which includes owning a castle in Scotland and a 200-acre farm near Romford which his parents run. Davis is one of the richest men in British sport.

LES DODD

Born: 11 February 1954, Southport, Merseyside, England

Turned professional: 1982

First ranking points: 1986 Rothmans Grand Prix

CAREER HIGHLIGHTS

1983
Embassy World Professional Championship (last 32)

1987
Tolly Cobbold English Professional Championship (runner-up)

Rankings
Year	Rank
1983	36
1984	43
1985	53
1986	69
1987	51
1988	62

The one-time 'heavyweight' of professional snooker, Les Dodd weighed in at 20 stone in 1986 but a visit to the local Weight-watchers Club had that reduced to 12½ stone in 12 months. The drop in weight coincided with an upturn in his fortunes.

A former amateur international, the ever-smiling Les turned professional in 1982 and reached the televised stage of the World Championship in his first season, but he lost narrowly 10-7 to seasoned campaigner Eddie Charlton. A succession of early knock-outs followed but in the English Professional Championship at Ipswich in March 1987 it came good for Les.

> **'I can't complain. I'm pleased for Les, he has been around a while and deserves some success.'**
>
> *Joe Johnson after Les beat him in the semi-final of the 1987 Tolly Ales English Professional Championship at Ipswich*

What a way to spend a birthday

After beating Tony Knowles, Barry West and Mike Hallett he enjoyed the best win of his career by beating world champion Joe Johnson in the semi-final. In the final, however, the occasion got the better of Dodd in the early stages and defending champion Tony Meo ran out the 9-5 winner. But consolation for Les, who celebrated his 33rd birthday during the final, came in the form of a £12,500 cheque – by far the biggest of his snooker career.

A former civil servant, Les started playing snooker as a teenager and was twice the civil service snooker champion. In order to play more snooker he quit the security of his office job and became a taxi driver.

After a promising amateur career in which he reached the northern final of the English Amateur Championship, he was accepted as a member of the WPBSA in 1982. He carried on taxi-driving in his early days as a professional.

After years of patience Les and his wife Christine are beginning to reap their rewards as Les no longer needs to drive the cab to supplement his income. Snooker can now provide Les, Chris and their three children with a comfortable living. His popularity and ability to entertain led to him working the 1987 summer season on the Pontins circuit, which he returned to in 1988.

During the 1987 Tennents UK Open he was on the brink of the biggest win of his career when he led Dennis Taylor 8-2 but lost 8-9.

Les Dodd shed nearly eight stone to win the Weight Watchers *Male Slimmer of the Year Award in 1988. The World Snooker Championship would make a nice double*

TONY DRAGO

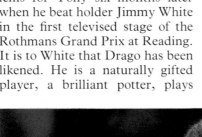

Born: 22 September 1965, Valetta, Malta

Turned professional: 1985

First ranking points: 1985 Rothmans Grand Prix

CAREER HIGHLIGHTS

1984
Malta Amateur Champion

1988
Embassy World Professional Championship
(quarter-final)

Rankings
1986   37
1987   32
1988   20

Tony Drago made a dramatic start to his professional career, picking up ranking points in the Rothmans Grand Prix and Coral UK Open. But in his second season, 1986-87, he truly established himself as a world-class player.

He gained ranking points in the first three tournaments of the season and in the Tennents UK Open beat Rex Williams, John Virgo and Willie Thorne before meeting Steve Davis in the quarter-final. Drago was given little or no chance against Davis, least of all by Thorne who said: 'Steve'll beat him 9-0'. But how wrong the man from Leicester was. Davis did win, but by only 9-8 and only after Drago 'threw' away the final frame. He led 54-1 but Davis put together a 41 break before missing the blue after the last red. Tony had an easy yellow to clear up the colours and win the match but nerves visibly got to him and Davis sneaked a win, thus preventing one of the game's biggest upsets.

A second Jimmy White? or a first Tony Drago?

If he was nervous in front of the television cameras on that occasion, there were no such prob-lems for Tony six months later when he beat holder Jimmy White in the first televised stage of the Rothmans Grand Prix at Reading. It is to White that Drago has been likened. He is a naturally gifted player, a brilliant potter, plays

Tony Drago, Malta's great snooker prospect, despite homesickness

aggressively and, like White, is very quick around the table. Willie Thorne, the man who gave Tony no chance against Steve Davis, once said about Tony: 'He is faster and more exciting than Jimmy White at the same age.'

It was in his home country that his talent was first spotted by Vic Harris, the man who said, when he saw Steve Davis at the age of 12, that he would be world champion one day. Harris had the same feeling about Drago after they played each other in Valetta. Tony won the Maltese Amateur title in 1984 and represented his country in that year's World Amateur Championship, where he established a new Championship record break of 132. Earlier in the year he had been accepted as a professional, but his application had been submitted in error and his name was withdrawn. The following year he made a *bona fide* application and was accepted.

Initially very homesick, between the start of the 1986-87 season and Christmas Tony flew back to Malta 11 times! More settled now, particularly after London club owner Neil Westfield became Tony's manager, Tony has taken a liking to English food. He beat Dennis Taylor to reach the quarter-final of the World Championship, before losing to Steve Davis.

'I never dreamed I would be meeting all these people and appearing on television.'

Tony's comments during his first year as a professional

'Today I beat my hero.'

After beating Jimmy White in the 1987 Rothmans. Tony used to mould his game on White, whom he used to watch for hours on television back home in Malta

---

STEVE DUGGAN

Born: 10 April 1958, Thurnscoe, Yorkshire, England

Turned professional: 1983

First ranking points: 1985 Goya Matchroom Trophy

CAREER HIGHLIGHTS

1982
Pontins Autumn Open Champion
WMC & IU Champion

1983
WMC & IU Champion

1985
Goya Matchroom Trophy (quarter-final)

Rankings
Year	Rank
1984	57
1985	70
1986	35
1987	37
1988	50

Regularly accompanying Stevie Duggan on the professional circuit are his two brothers, Jim and Jack. Both are useful players themselves, and capable of 50/60 breaks; if there was such a thing as a family triples competition, there would be few in the country who could touch the Duggan lads.

South Yorkshireman Steve joined the professional ranks in 1983 after a great couple of years as one of the top amateur players. In 1982 he won the competitive WMC & IU Championship for his Thurnscoe club, and the same year won the Pontins Autumn Open and gained England international honours. A successful professional career was being predicted for Steve, and after retaining the WMC & IU title (only the third man since 1945 to retain it) he turned professional.

Steve beats two former world champions

The first two years for Duggan were disastrous and he slipped to 70th in the rankings, but he started his third professional season with a bang. He beat Fred Davis, Ray Reardon, Ian Black and Willie Thorne to reach the quarter-final of the Goya Matchroom Trophy and, despite losing 5-2 to Cliff Thorburn, Steve picked up his first ranking points, which helped elevate him to 35th in the world. For that one performance Steve collected a cheque for £5,250; it was nearly three times his total winnings from the previous season! Although he did not collect any more ranking points that season, he had overcome the mental barrier and convinced himself he was a winner and was no longer a regular casualty in the qualifying rounds of the major events.

Four more ranking points in the 1986-87 season saw the methodical Steve approach the top 32, his best win being over Neal Foulds in the Mercantile Credit Classic. Steve practises for four or five hours a day at the Woodlands near Doncaster.

At last it seems to be coming good for the quiet lad from Yorkshire and his wife Julie, who has supported Steve through his darker days on the professional circuit. She stays at home when Steve is playing, but still encourages him. She leaves Jim and Jack to put in an appearance on behalf of the family.

One third of the snooker-playing Duggan brothers – Steve. After a great amateur career Steve turned professional in 1983

RAY EDMONDS

Born: 28 May 1936, Cleethorpes, Lincolnshire, England

Turned professional: 1978

First ranking points: 1985 Rothmans Grand Prix

CAREER HIGHLIGHTS

1969
English Amateur Champion

1971
WMC & IU Champion

1972
WMC & IU Champion
World Amateur Champion

1974
English Amateur Champion
World Amateur Champion

1985
World Professional Billiards Champion

Rankings

Year	Ranking
1983	34
1984	50
1985	51
1986	46
1987	59
1988	55

In his amateur days Ray Edmonds showed great skill and nerve, qualities which won him two English amateur titles, and two world titles. Sadly that promise was never fulfilled when he joined the professional ranks.

His first professional tournament gave indications that his successful amateur career would continue, when he reached the last eight of the Coral UK Championship before losing to Bill Werbeniuk 9-8. But, apart from reaching the semi-final of the English Professional Championship in 1981, when he lost 9-0 to Steve Davis, Ray's record in the professional game has nowhere near matched his great amateur career.

Edmonds wins all the top amateur tournaments

Now better known for his billiards than snooker, it is surprising that Ray entered the English Amateur Billiards Championship only once, and at the time of his turning professional in 1978 his only competitive billiards had been in the Lincolnshire and Humberside areas. In those days he was outstanding as a snooker player and was runner-up in the English Amateur Championship in 1961. In 1969 he beat Jonathan Barron to win the title and over the next five years Ray was to appear in three finals. He lost to Jonathan Barron in 1972, and to Marcus Owen a year later but in 1974 he beat Patsy Fagan 11-7 as he appeared in a record-equalling fifth final.

The English amateur title is one of the most coveted titles in the amateur game. The other prestige non-professional titles are the world title and the WMC & IU championship. Ray added to his impressive list of successes by winning each of those titles twice.

He won his first WMC & IU title in 1971 when playing for the Skegness WMC, and a year later he retained the title. That same year he beat South Africa's Mannie Francisco, brother of Silvino and father of Peter, in the World Championship final at Cardiff. It was a close affair with Edmonds running out the 11-10 winner, and also making the championship's top break of 101. He retained his world title at Dublin two years later when he beat Welshman Geoff Thomas 11-9 in the final to become the second man to retain it.

As an amateur Ray Edmonds was twice world snooker champion, but since turning professional he has had more success at billiards

Edmonds has his own road

After his second world title Grimsby Council decided to name a road after Ray in recognition of his achievement, and so was born Edmonds Way. He is believed to be the only snooker personality to have a road named after him.

There are few players with a better amateur record than Ray Edmonds and to complete his list of honours he represented England in the very first Home International match, against Wales at Port Talbot in 1969; between then and his turning professional in 1978 he appeared in every international series. Since turning professional, however, the best result for the former paint salesman has not been at snooker, but at billiards when in 1985 he lifted the World Professional title at the Hatton Garden Snooker Centre. Three times a losing semi-finalist, it came good for Ray when he beat Norman Dagley, making his professional debut, 3-1 in the final.

When not playing Ray is still involved with the sport, either via his own snooker centre, the Ray Edmonds Snooker Centre in Grimsby, which he runs with the help of his son Michael, or via the microphone as one of the respected summarisers for the ITV commentary team. He also owns a race horse, Ray with Words.

ALLISON FISHER

Born: 24 February 1968, Peacehaven, Sussex, England

CAREER HIGHLIGHTS

1985
Women's World Amateur Champion
UK Women's National Champion

1986
Women's World Champion

1987
Tuborg Women's UK Champion

Allison Fisher stands a very good chance of making snooker history in the not too distant future by becoming the first female member of the governing body, the World Professional Billiards and Snooker Association (WPBSA).

First of all though, Allison has got to prove that she is more than the best female player in the world, by competing against, and beating, the top male non-professionals in the pro-ticket qualifying series. She came close in the 1986-87 series when she finished just outside the qualifying top eight.

An all-round sportswoman, Allison first became interested in snooker after watching 'Pot Black' at the age of seven. She received a 2-foot snooker table that Christmas and then her uncle gave her his 6-foot table. At the age of 12 she played on her first full-size table, at the Peacehaven Central Club. A year later she was the only female member of the Lewes League. In 1984 she became the first woman to represent East Sussex in the Inter-Counties Championship. Despite spending a lot of time playing snooker, Allison never neglected her studies and completed her education at the Tideway Comprehensive school, coming out with 5 O-levels in 1984.

A great talent spotted

Cheerfulness and dedication are Allison's trademarks. Her immense talent was spotted by expert coach and television commentator, Jim Meadowcroft. She also sought advice from Frank Callan, the man who has acted as mentor to Steve Davis, John Parrott and Terry Griffiths. Allison openly admits to modelling her game on Davis's, and she has certainly become the Steve Davis of the women's game. Indeed, after losing to Stacey Hillyard in the Women's World Amateur Championship in 1984, she did not lose to another woman until the 1987 World Championship, when Stacey beat her again, in the semi-final.

Allison's sole ambition is to become the first female member of the WPBSA. She is being helped by many people in that quest, not least her parents, who built an extension on their Sussex home in order to house a full-size table. Metro Computers of Kent have also helped Allison with a three-year sponsorship deal, and manager Frank Sandell has guided her. With that backing, and her own great talent, there is no reason why Allison Fisher's dream should not be fulfilled.

Posing with the world professional trophy. Will she be the first woman to win it?

'I've got past the stage of being treated as a lady player. I'm just another player.'

NEAL FOULDS

Born: 13 July 1963, Perivale, Middlesex, England

Turned professional: 1983

First ranking points: 1984 Embassy World Professional Championship

In just four years as a professional Neal Foulds climbed to number three in the world, behind fellow Londoners Steve Davis and Jimmy White. The dramatic rise gave pleasure to one man more than any other – Neal's dad Geoff.

Geoff Foulds is a very good snooker player in his own right, but he neglected his own game once he realised Neal's potential, and has since had great pleasure watching Neal progress from leading amateur to leading professional in five years.

Neal arrived on the professional scene tipped as the man to succeed Steve Davis as world champion, and when he beat Alex Higgins on his debut at the Crucible in 1984 there was every sign that that prediction would soon be turned into

---

'I see Neal as a definite top-eight player.'

. . . so said Barry Hearn the day he signed him. Within 18 months he was a top-three player

For relaxation in the summer months you will see Neal sitting at Lord's with a bottle of pop and some sandwiches watching his favourite cricket team, Middlesex

---

reality. His run in the championship was halted by Doug Mountjoy in the next round, but Neal ended his first season by jumping to number 30 in the rankings. He showed great coolness in front of the television cameras at the Crucible, which obviously stemmed from his experience gained in appearing on 'Junior Pot Black' in 1981.

Help from Ron Gross

Neal picked up his first cue at the Greenford Conservative Club when he was 11 years of age. Bespectacled at the time, he started wearing contact lenses when he was 16, and that change immediately brought about an improvement in his game. He started work as a clerk with the Pro-

Neal Foulds had a disastrous season in 1987–8 but he is too good to be 'down' for long and should re-emerge as a threat soon

CAREER HIGHLIGHTS

1982
National Under-19 Champion

1984
Pontins Open Champion

1986
BCE International Champion

1987
Embassy World Professional
Championship (semi-final)

1988
World Cup (member of
winning England side)

Rankings

Year	Rank	Year	Rank
1984	30	1987	3
1985	23	1988	3
1986	13		

vident Capital Insurance company at Shepherds Bush, but that lasted only nine months. Geoff put Neal in touch with Ron Gross for extra coaching in 1981. Between the pair of them they helped develop Neal's natural talents and turn him into one of the best young players in the London area. Ron had him working at his Neasden club, and paid him the same wages he had been picking up from the Provident.

Neal left school with two O-levels, and reflects how most of his schoolmates ended up on the dole; Neal won £40,000 in his first professional season. Snooker was always foremost in Neal's mind and when he reached the final of the National Under-19 Championship in 1982, where he beat his current rival John Parrott, Neal was already playing snooker full time. He went on to make his England international debut that year and in 1983 applied for and was given professional status.

No titles, but close . . .

He built on that great first year by climbing seven places up the rankings in 1984-85. Although he did not win a title, he proved he was capable of living with the best players in the world. Neal had a great run in the Rothmans Grand Prix, where he beat Willie Thorne and Tony Knowles before reaching the semi-final. Dennis Taylor prevented Neal's first appearance in a final and it took great players like Terry Griffiths, Alex Higgins, Jimmy White and Steve Davis to thwart Neal's progress in other major events. And apart from Higgins' 5-1 win in the Dulux, they had to battle to beat the youngster. He took White to 9-7 in the English Professional Championship and in the Embassy was engaged in a great first-round

One of the favourites for the 1987 World Championship, Neal was beaten in the semi-final

battle with Davis which the champion won 10-8.

Neal enjoyed a great third season when he climbed into the top 16 after picking up 12 ranking points. It all started in the Goya Matchroom Trophy at Trentham Gardens, when he reached the semi-final before losing to Jimmy White. Doug Mountjoy ended Neal's chances of a second semi-final appearance in the Mercantile

Against his dad

Neal Foulds has played his dad Geoff only twice since they became professionals and won both times.

| 1986 Tolly Cobbold English Professional Championship | Third round | 9-4 |
| 1986 BCE International | Fourth round | 5-0 |

. . . on each occasion Neal went on to the final.

A younger Neal Foulds seen with the man who has been his inspiration, father Geoff

Credit Classic but in the non-ranking Tolly Cobbold English Professional Championship Neal eventually reached his first professional final. In the first round snooker history was made when Neal and father Geoff were drawn together. Neal won the family battle 9-4 and then went on to beat Ray Edmonds, Jimmy White and Mike Hallett in a great semi-final that went the full 17 frames. Neal's title ambitions ended when Meo ran out the 9-7 winner in the final.

Neal failed to progress beyond the first round of the Embassy again when this time Tony Knowles beat him 10-9, but Neal could not call his season anything but successful. If that was successful, however, the 1986-87 season was outstanding.

Joins Hearn – wins first title

He had become the sixth member of the Barry Hearn Matchroom team earlier in 1986 and that was a tremendous boost to his morale. Geoff had previously handled Neal's affairs but his son was getting too big for him to look after. Mark McCormack's IMG organisation approached them with a view to Neal being their first snooker client, but they turned McCormack down, flattered as they were, and went to Hearn.

Neal's great season started with him having another good run at Trentham Gardens, this time in the BCE International. He beat dad 5-0 in the fourth round before reaching the final after a terrific semi-final battle with Eugene Hughes, which Neal won 9-8. In the final Canadian Cliff Thorburn provided the opposition but the youngster kept cool and won 12-9, collecting a first prize of £35,000 in

the process. But that was only the start of a season that took Neal to number three in the world.

He beat Willie Thorne and Tony Meo on the way to a semi-final meeting with Rex Williams in the next ranking tournament, the Rothmans Grand Prix. After a great 17-frame battle, Williams ran out the winner by just one frame. But Foulds' season was far from over.

He reached the final of the Tennents UK Open at the Preston Guildhall and on the way beat Jimmy White 9-7 before surprisingly easy wins over Cliff Thorburn and John Parrott. He then came up against Steve Davis in the final and the 'Master' came out on top 16-7.

Defeats by Stevie Duggan and Ken Owers at the first hurdle of the Mercantile and Tolly Ales English Professional Championship respectively were the only flaws in an otherwise perfect season for Foulds. He returned to winning form in the New Year by reaching the final of the Dulux British Open at Derby but it was Jimmy White who proved Neal's stumbling block once more as the man from Tooting won 13-9.

As the world championship came around Neal was obviously being tipped as one of the favourites, but Joe Johnson was not going to let go of his crown lightly, and beat him 16-9 in the semi final.

In 1988, a disappointing season, he lost to Terry Griffiths in the quarter-finals, but previously had helped England win the Fersina World Cup.

Neal Foulds comes from a very closely knit family consisting of his mother and father (Pat and Geoff) and his sister Susie. Neal is married to Janet, they have a son Darren, and Neal does not like the flamboyant lifestyle of some of his fellow professionals. He does allow himself to indulge in greyhound racing and in 1986 he became an owner. All his dogs' names are prefixed with 'Greenfield' and are trained by Les Dickson at Windsor. The best is Greenfield Game.

DANNY FOWLER

Born: 30 July 1956, Worksop, Nottinghamshire, England

Turned professional: 1984

First ranking points: 1985 Rothmans Grand Prix

CAREER HIGHLIGHTS

1987
*Mercantile Credit Classic
(last 16)
Tennents United Kingdom
Open (last 16)*

Rankings
1985	55
1986	33
1987	40
1988	43

Although he gained English international honours in 1983, the amateur career of Danny Fowler was not outstanding in terms of championship successes but, as one of the top quality players based at the North Midlands Snooker Centre in Worksop, he developed into a very competitive money player.

The first bin man to win the world title?

A former miner and local council worker in the refuse department, Danny is a very attacking player and has great cue power. No doubt many hours watching Alex Higgins have helped Danny develop his style. He started playing snooker at 15 but when he was 20 gave up the game for a couple of years. Then, with the boom in snooker, he started playing again seriously. He was one of 15 new

Danny Fowler in action against Terry Griffiths in 1986

professionals accepted as members of the WPBSA in May 1984. At the time Danny was based at the Ashfield Snooker Centre, Sutton-in-Ashfield, Nottinghamshire. He is now the resident professional at the Grove Mill Snooker Centre in Retford and is managed by local businessman Tony Goulding.

Picking up merit points for his performances in the Jameson, Coral UK Open and Mercantile Credit Classic, Danny ended his first professional season in mid-order in the rankings in 55th place. A 9-6 win over Neal Foulds in the Coral was one of his best results of

---

'My game is all right but I've got to find out whether I have the extra confidence to beat the better players.'

Danny before his match with Terry Griffiths in the 1986 World Championship. Griffiths won 10-2

---

the season and when it came to the World Championship Danny inflicted 10-0 whitewashes on John Hargreaves and Jim Donnelly. His progress was being watched with interest, but John Parrott brought him down to earth in the next round by beating him 10-2.

Hong Kong tour

Danny jumped 22 places up the rankings the following season. He picked up ranking points in the Rothmans, where he beat his Worksop pal Bill Werbeniuk 5-1 before, on his television debut, Steve Davis beat him 5-1. In the Coral he beat Perrie Mans 9-2, and in the Embassy, making his Crucible debut, Danny lost 10-2 to the former champion Terry Griffiths. During the summer of 1986 Danny and Bill Werbeniuk toured Hong Kong and played local amateur players as part of a sponsorship deal with San Miguel beers organised by Tony Goulding.

The 1986-87 season started disastrously for Danny but then he reached the last 16 of the Mercantile Credit Classic after great wins over Tony Knowles and Mike Hallett. Then Stephen Hendry won their fifth-round match by the odd frame in nine when Danny missed a normally easy black after sinking great pressure pots on the brown, blue and pink. Hendry was set up, and went on to win.

In 1987-88 Danny reached the final 16 of the Tennents UK Championship.

PETER FRANCISCO

Born: 14 February 1962, Cape Town, South Africa

Turned professional: 1984

First ranking points: 1985 Rothmans Grand Prix

Peter Francisco has certainly maintained the high standard the Francisco family has established in the snooker world over the years.

His uncle Silvino is a current fellow professional and Peter's father (Silvino's brother) Mannie was a leading South African player for many years; he was South African amateur billiards champion 13 times between 1959 and 1977 and was six times the Snooker Champion. He also came close to a rare double when he was runner-up in the World Amateur Billiards and Snooker Championships in successive years.

Followed in father's footsteps

Peter, a fluent potter, followed his father and won both the South African billiards and snooker titles before his acceptance as a professional by the WPBSA in 1984. Since then Peter has developed into a world-class player and is rapidly catching up with Silvino in the ranking list.

His first professional season passed with little to report but then he got a job as the resident professional at the Clacton Snooker Centre and that coincided with his improved form. After a disappointing first-hurdle elimination by Matt Gibson in the Goya, Peter picked up two ranking points for reaching the fifth round of the Rothmans Grand Prix before Terry Griffiths eliminated

Peter Francisco, South Africa's number two, nephew of Silvino

---

'It's nice for a non-swimmer to sink a Portuguese man-of-war.'

Alex Higgins after beating Peter in the 1986 Dulux, and making reference to Francisco's Portuguese ancestry

---

him. Steve Davis beat him in the fifth round of the Mercantile Credit Classic, but another two ranking points were collected, and he picked up two more in the Dulux British Open. This time Alex Higgins dented Francisco's ambitions of progressing any further. On his way to the fifth round, however, Peter had the best win of his career to date when he beat Jimmy White 5-4. The season ended with Francisco narrowly failing to make his Crucible debut when Neal Foulds beat him 10-9 at the final qualifying stage.

Two meetings with uncle Silvino

Peter's vast improvement continued the following season and in reaching the semi-final of the BCE International at Stoke-on-Trent he reached the highest point of his professional career.

After beating both Alex Higgins (in the fourth round) and the Canadian Marcel Gauvreau, he set up a quarter-final meeting with his uncle. Silvino had beaten Peter in the semi-final of the South African

Professional Championship during the summer, but this time it was Peter who came out on top, 5-3. In his semi-final, Francisco pushed top Canadian Cliff Thorburn all the way before losing 9-7. Peter's only other performance of note that season was in the Mercantile Credit Classic, where he beat world champion Joe Johnson before losing to Silvino in the fifth round.

The climb up the rankings continued in 1987-88 and Peter stopped doubting his own ability. He equalled his previous best performance by reaching the semi-final of the Rothmans Grand Prix at Reading. He beat Joe Johnson, Graham Cripsey and Willie Thorne before Willie's team-mate Dennis Taylor eliminated Francisco at the last-four stage.

A member of the Francisco family has held the honour of being the highest ranked South African since 1984. That honour has fallen to Silvino up to now. The way things are going, it could soon be his nephew, Peter.

CAREER HIGHLIGHTS

1981
South Africa Amateur Snooker Champion

1982
South Africa Amateur Snooker Champion
South Africa Amateur Billiards Champion

1983
South Africa Amateur Snooker Champion

1986
BCE International (semi-final)

1987
Rothmans Grand Prix (semi-final)

Rankings
1985	59
1986	26
1987	18
1988	14

SILVINO FRANCISCO

Born: 3 May 1946, Cape Town, South Africa

Turned professional: 1978

*First ranking points: 1982 Embassy World Professional
Championship*

Silvino Francisco had been a professional for four years before he made his first visit to England in 1982 for the Embassy World Professional Championship. And he nearly caused a sensation. Based in Leicester at the time, Silvino stayed with Willie Thorne and his mum. After beating Chris Ross 9-0 and Paddy Morgan 9-1 in the qualifying competition, Silvino reached the Crucible stage at his first attempt. His first opponent there was the former finalist Dennis Taylor, but Francisco was not overawed and won 10-7. He beat youngster Dean Reynolds 13-8 in the next round and suddenly there was talk of him being South Africa's first world

'I'm very glad of this, it made me a living.'

Silvino showing gratitude to Pontins for allowing him to play the holiday camp circuit when he first decided to settle in England

champion. But that dream, and the talk, stopped when former champion Ray Reardon won their quarter-final clash. But the name of Silvino Francisco suddenly became well known in snooker circles.

Dennis Taylor gained revenge by beating Silvino 10-9 in the first round at Sheffield the following year. After that championship

Francisco decided to quit his job as an executive with a South African oil company and to set up a home in England and play the tournament circuit regularly. During the summer he got a job on the Pontins exhibition circuit and was grateful for being given the chance to make a living out of doing something he enjoyed – playing snooker.

Silvino is not the only snooker playing Francisco

Silvino's father, a Portuguese fisherman, sold his boat and moved to Cape Town where he bought a restaurant. There were two snooker tables in the restaurant and Silvino started playing when he was nine. His older brother Mannie showed early promise and also went on to become a top class billiards and snooker player in South Africa. Although Mannie has now turned his attention to bowls, he was the runner-up in the World Amateur Billiards final to

Silvino Francisco (with trophy) after beating Kirk Stevens to win the 1985 Dulux British Open

Silvino Francisco is now South Africa's leading player

Norman Dagley in 1971 and the following year was runner-up to Ray Edmonds in the World Amateur Snooker Championship, despite leading 7-0 at one stage.

The two brothers both competed in the 1976 World Amateur Championship in Johannesburg and they were drawn together in the quarter-final. Silvino won 5-1 but was beaten 8-2 in the semifinal by the eventual champion Doug Mountjoy. Before he joined the oil company Silvino worked for 14 years for Thurston's in South Africa, and is one of the few professional players who could assemble a snooker table as well as play on it. He made the decision to turn professional in 1978 because of the political restriction on sportsmen in South Africa. Francisco is now based in Chesterfield with his second wife Denise, who presented him with a son, Ashley, just two weeks before Christmas 1986.

'I wouldn't have gone home with any money at all if it hadn't been for Willie and his mum.'

Silvino commenting that most of his £3,500 prize-money from the 1982 World Championship went on expenses . . . only Willie Thorne and his mum helped stop him from making a loss

---

A well deserved first title

The previous year Silvino enjoyed his greatest moment in snooker when he won his first major event, the Dulux British Open. Wins over Jimmy White, Tony Meo and Alex Higgins put him in the final against Kirk Stevens. It was the first major final in which a Briton did not appear and both men were seeking their first win in a ranking event. Stevens started favourite, particularly after beating Dennis Taylor, and then Steve Davis in the semifinal. But on the day Silvino came out on top by 12-9. Most of his winnings went on putting an extension on his Chesterfield home to house a snooker table.

That win, however, sparked off a controversial spell in the career of Silvino Francisco. He made allegations that Stevens was playing while under the influence of illegal stimulants. His claims were picked up by a newspaper, and resulted in Francisco being fined a then-record £6,000 by the WPBSA, and suffering the loss of two ranking points. Shortly afterwards, Stevens revealed in a story in a rival newspaper that he had been taking drugs. Francisco appealed against his fine and, after much legal haggling, the fine was returned and his ranking points reinstated.

Despite those troubles Silvino lost few friends on the professional circuit as he remained one of its most popular members. Sadly, it looked as though the troubles were affecting his game, but in 1986-87, with the affair behind him, he had one of his best seasons and improved to number 10 in the rankings by reaching the semi-final of the Rothmans Grand Prix and quarter-final of the Mercantile Credit Classic. But in the World Championship he fell in the second round to Mike Hallett. Since his glorious Crucible debut in 1982 Silvino has never managed to get beyond two stages of the competition.

CAREER HIGHLIGHTS

1968-69
South Africa Amateur Snooker Champion

1972
South Africa Amateur Billiards Champion

1973
South Africa Amateur Billiards Champion

1974
South Africa Amateur Snooker Champion

1975
South Africa Amateur Billiards Champion

1977
South Africa Amateur Snooker Champion

1985
Dulux British Open Champion

1986
South Africa Professional Snooker Champion

Rankings

Year	Ranking
1983	21
1984	17
1985	13
1986	12
1987	10
1988	12

LEN GANLEY

Born: Lurgan, near Belfast, Northern Ireland

Top referee Len Ganley

Len Ganley visited his sister in Burton-on-Trent in 1971. The visit was scheduled to last ten days . . . he hasn't gone back yet! Now settled in the town, Len worked as a milkman and bus driver for a while before taking up snooker refereeing full-time. He had been refereeing in Ireland for many years – his qualifications were not recognised in England but he soon gained the necessary qualifications as laid down by the B & SCC. In 1979 he gained his Grade A certificate.

Best break 136

A proficient snooker player as well as referee, he started playing in the Lurgan, Lisburn and Belfast League. He continued playing, as well as refereeing, when he moved to England and won the Burton and South Derbyshire title twice. His highest break is a creditable 136. Now a full-time professional referee, Len covers all the major tournaments and is called on to go on major tours by the Matchroom team and others.

One of his first great moments as a referee was the 1983 World Championship final between Steve Davis and Cliff Thorburn but the match he enjoyed controlling most was the 1983 Coral UK final between Davis and Alex Higgins, when Higgins came back from 7-0 to win a remarkable match 16-15.

MARCEL GAUVREAU

Born: 9 January 1955, Little Moose, Saskatchewan, Canada

Turned professional: 1983

First ranking points: 1984 Jameson International

Marcel Gauvreau, like the other Canadians, is a tough competitor to beat and he never acknowledges a match is over until the players shake hands. He found it difficult to adjust to a new life in Britain in 1984 but has now successfully made the transition.

A five-hour epic

A good future in the professional game looked assured for Marcel after he reached the Crucible stage of the Embassy in his first season and when, in the opening ranking tournament of 1984-85, the Jameson, he beat John Parrott and Kirk Stevens (5-1) before losing to Willie Thorne. But he never got beyond the second round of any tournament after that until the 1986 Mercantile Credit, when he booked a last-16 meeting with Jimmy White after an epic battle with Irishman Paddy Browne that started at 3 pm and did not finish until 5½ hours later, at an average 41 minutes per frame. Against White, Marcel fared well, and was only 3-2 down at one time, but the Englishman ran out the 5-2 winner.

The only other last-16 appearance for Marcel was in the BCE International at Trentham Gardens, also in 1986. He reached the fifth round by beating Ray Reardon 5-2 before Peter Francisco spoilt Gauvreau's ambitions at the next stage. They were Gauvreau's only ranking points of the season as he slipped slightly down the rankings, but he has the ability to arrest that situation and start moving up again.

CAREER HIGHLIGHTS

1986
Mercantile Credit Classic (last 16)
BCE International (last 16)

Rankings

Year	Ranking
1983	—
1984	—
1985	39
1986	38
1987	42
1988	63

Gritty Canadian, Marcel Gauvreau

DAVE GILBERT

Born: 15 August 1961, Bethnal Green, London, England

Turned professional: 1985

First ranking points: 1987 Fidelity Unit Trusts International

CAREER HIGHLIGHTS

1979
Pontins Junior Champion

1987
Fidelity Unit Trusts International (last 16)

Rankings
1986   72
1987   82
1988   57

The world of Dave Gilbert was shattered in 1980. Travelling from his London home to the Pontins Tournament at Prestatyn he was involved in a head-on collision on the M6 near Stafford. Dave's sister Sue was tragically killed. He was fortunate to get away with his life, but he had to have a steel plate inserted in his left arm and it looked as though his snooker days were over. A year earlier he had beaten John Parrott to win the Pontins Junior title. Suddenly a great talent seemed lost.

A gritty and determined player, that same determination came through as he lay in hospital and, with the 100 per cent support of his parents, Les and Brenda, East Ender Dave fought his way back and soon became the 'Steve Davis of the amateur game'. He was the man to beat.

Snooker yes: Smithfield and Hatton Garden . . . no!

Les Gilbert was a London Transport bus driver and introduced Dave to snooker at the London Transport garage where Patsy Fagan played a lot of his early snooker. It was obvious after a couple of jobs at Smithfield meat market and as an engraver at Hatton Garden that the only job Dave wanted was to play snooker

for a living. Ron Shore at the Ilford Snooker Centre took him under his wing and in 1983 he beat Terry Whitthread in the final of the London Championship, giving the first signs that he was re-establishing himself as a leading player.

Dave took up his professional status in July 1985 after being rejected the previous year. But the transition was not easy and his excellent amateur record counted for nothing. He met his wife Toni in 1986 and they were married soon afterwards; she has since been a great influence on him.

The first real taste of success for Dave came in the 1987 Fidelity Unit Trusts International at Trentham Gardens when he reached the fifth round and picked up his first ranking points after beating Cliff Wilson on his television debut. Despite not being able to straighten his left arm at the elbow, two victims in the Fidelity, Dave Martin and Cliff Wilson, will confirm it does not affect the snooker playing ability of this up-and-coming youngster.

Former Hatton Garden engraver Dave Gilbert is now carving a name for himself in the world of snooker

---

'It needs the occasional 3-in-1 oiling.'

Dave referring to the steel plate in his left arm

'He's a snooker player, be careful how you put his arms together.'

Barry Hearn, to doctors at Bart's Hospital after Dave's car crash

NIGEL GILBERT

Born: 20 March 1959, Bedford, England

Turned professional: 1986

First ranking points: 1987 Fidelity Unit Trusts International

CAREER HIGHLIGHTS

1987
Fidelity Unit Trust
International (last 16)

Rankings
1987   99
1988   56

Nigel Gilbert became a professional in 1986, but he only just scraped into the senior ranks via the back door after finishing ninth in the 1985 Pro-Ticket series. The top eight were eligible to take up professional status but one of those eight, Terry Whitthread, had already been accepted as a professional and it meant Nigel jumping a place and becoming eligible to join the professional ranks.

Nigel was introduced to snooker at the age of 16 by a local Bedford butcher and it was not long before school took second place to the new love of his life. It was at the Greyfriars Club, owned by Mick Fisher, that Nigel started to develop into a leading amateur. Regular play against Fisher helped improve his game considerably. After leaving school Nigel worked on the market stalls before getting a trade behind him and he served his apprenticeship as an electrician with the London Brick Company. He eventually got the sack for poor time-keeping . . . he hasn't had a job since.

Timekeeping . . . not Nigel's best asset

Gilbert was reminded of his poor time-keeping record during the qualifying rounds of the 1987 Mercantile Credit Classic at the Norbreck Castle Hotel in Blackpool. To avoid travelling he stayed at the venue and he was late in arriving for his match with Jimmy van Rensburg and was penalised three frames. He lost 5-3 and still maintains to this day his watch was wrong.

A fine attacking player, Nigel wears a glove on his bridging hand because he perspires a lot. Television viewers got the opportunity to see this rare sight when he made two appearances in the 1987 Fidelity at Stoke-on-Trent, where he reached the fifth round and collected the first ranking points of his career, before losing 5-0 to Eddie Charlton.

The improved confidence Nigel showed at the start of his second season was all too obvious and he is going to be one to watch over the next few years. A new sponsorship deal with Jo-Jo UK Limited has helped boost his confidence even further.

Nigel Gilbert, complete with glove on his bridging hand which he wears to combat perspiration

TERRY GRIFFITHS

Born: 16 October 1947, Llanelli, Carmarthenshire, Wales

Turned professional: 1978

First ranking points: 1979 Embassy World Professional Championship

Although he did not realise it at the time, losing to Steve Newbury in the quarter-final of the Welsh Amateur Championship in 1978 was the best thing that happened to Terry Griffiths. It was Griffiths' ambition to play in that year's World Amateur Championship in Malta but he needed to win the Welsh title to quality.

Newbury ended that dream and Griffiths immediately turned professional. Twelve months later Griffiths was crowned World Professional Champion and not Amateur Champion as he had set his sights on the year before . . . and it was all thanks to losing to Steve Newbury.

Although he had been playing

CAREER HIGHLIGHTS

1975
Welsh Amateur Champion

1977-78
English Amateur Champion

1979
Embassy World Professional Champion
State Express World Team Classic (member of winning Wales team)

1980
Benson & Hedges Masters Champion
Benson & Hedges Irish Masters Champion
State Express World Team Classic (member of winning Wales team)

1981
Benson & Hedges Irish Masters Champion

1982
Lada Classic Champion
Benson & Hedges Irish Masters Champion
Coral UK Champion

1985
Welsh Professional Champion

1986
Welsh Professional Champion
BCE Belgian Classic Champion

1988
Welsh Professional Champion

Rankings

Year	Ranking
1983	9
1984	8
1985	8
1986	10
1987	6
1988	5

The 1979 world champion Terry Griffiths lines up an awkward shot. One of the biggest winners in the early 1980s, Griffiths remains among snooker's elite despite not winning a major tournament since the 1982 Coral UK Championship

Terry Griffiths holds aloft the World Championship trophy (and cheque)
after beating Dennis Taylor to win the title in 1979

'I've never been so chuffed in all my life, not even winning the World Championship.'

After watching his son Wayne win the Llanelli championship in 1987

'Does this mean you're as good as Ray Reardon now?'

That's what Wayne asked his dad after he won the 1979 world title

snooker since he was a teenager, and at 16 was the Llanelli and District Champion, he didn't start playing the game seriously until he was 25, when he appeared in his first Welsh Championship, losing to Geoff Thomas in the final. But after that Terry had an outstanding amateur career.

He avenged that defeat by Thomas in the 1975 Welsh final and thus qualified for the 1976 World Championship in Johannesburg. He lost to Jimmy Van Rensburg in the quarter-final, as fellow Welshman Doug Mountjoy went on to win the title.

English Amateur champion

Terry beat Sid Hood 13-3 to win the English Amateur title in 1977 and that year lost to Alex Higgins in the final of the Pontins Open at Prestatyn. Terry had been a regular member of the Welsh international team since 1973-74 and lost only two matches in 14 appearances in the Home International series. After retaining the English title in 1978, when he beat Joe Johnson 13-6, Terry turned professional.

Griffiths seemed poised to spring a surprise in his first professional event, the 1978 Coral UK Championship at Preston, when he led Rex Williams 8-2 before Rex staged a remarkable recovery to win 9-8. But Terry's greatest moment was to come in the Embassy World Championship at Sheffield. He had to beat Bernard Bennett and Jim Meadowcroft to qualify but once at the Crucible he overcame some of the game's biggest names to reach the final.

Perrie Mans was his first victim. Alex Higgins was Terry's next scalp, but what a contest it was, with Griffiths winning 13-12. Another great match followed in the semi-final when Griffiths beat Australian Eddie Charlton 19-17 in a match that finished in the early hours of the morning.

The final was a Wales versus Ireland affair, with Dennis Taylor standing between Terry and a momentous victory. Both men were searching for their first major professional win. Terry won 24-16, and in doing so became the fourth man after Joe Davis, John Spencer and Alex Higgins to win the title at his first attempt.

Team-mate of Davis, but still deadly rivals

Over the next three years Terry, along with Steve Davis, dominated the game. Terry and Steve became team-mates under Barry Hearn's shrewd management, and in 1981 Hearn managed the number 2 and 3 players in the world.

Before 1979 was out Terry reached the final of the Coral UK Championship, but lost 14-13 to John Virgo. He was also a member of the Welsh team that won the first World Cup competition. Higgins

Terry Griffiths with Frank Callan, coach extraordinaire and mentor to many top players

His record in the Benson and Hedges

Between 1980 and 1984 Terry Griffiths had a remarkable record of reaching eight of the ten finals in either the Benson & Hedges Masters or Benson & Hedges Irish Masters, as follows:

Masters		Irish Masters	
1980	beat Alex Higgins 9-5	beat Doug Mountjoy	9-8
1981	lost to Alex Higgins 6-9	beat Ray Reardon	9-7
1982	lost to Steve Davis 5-9	beat Steve Davis	9-5
1983	lost in quarter-final	lost in semi-final	
1984	lost to Jimmy White 5-9	lost to Steve Davis	1-9

After beating Ray Reardon 7-3 in an all-Welsh final Terry Griffiths won the 1983 Pontins Open trophy at the Prestatyn Camp

and Doug Mountjoy fell to Terry as he won the Benson & Hedges Masters and Irish Masters titles in 1980 but in the World Championship it was a first-round exit to Steve Davis. Davis inflicted an embarrassing 9-0 defeat on Griffiths in the Coral later in the year and Davis proved to be the bogeyman again in the 1981 World Championship when he won their quarter-final clash 13-9.

Davis stamped his authority on the game, and on Terry, in the final of the 1981 Coral UK Championship with an emphatic 16-3 win.

However, in the first tournament of 1982, Griffiths, after beating Cliff Thorburn and Alex Higgins each by 5-1 to reach the final of the Lada Classic, avenged those defeats by Davis by beating the Londoner 9-8 in a great final. The two men met again in the finals of the Benson & Hedges Masters and Yamaha International, with the honours going back to Davis, but Griffiths won 9-5 when they met in the final of the Irish Masters in 1982.

On his way to winning the Coral UK title in 1982 Terry beat Davis 9-6 before a memorable final with Higgins which Griffiths won 16-15. Since then Terry has not won a ranking tournament, although he has twice won the

Welsh Professional title and in 1986 won the first major professional snooker event in Europe when he won the BCE Belgian Classic by beating Kirk Stevens 9-7 in the final. Despite his lack of recent wins Terry has had no problem maintaining his top-16 ranking.

Another snooker talent in the Griffiths household

A relaxed Terry Griffiths had his best season for a long time in 1987-88, reaching the final of the World Championship, beating Jimmy White in the semi-final. He lost to Steve Davis, who on four previous occasions had beaten him at the quarter-final stage.

A former apprentice blacksmith, postman, bus conductor and insurance salesman, Terry married wife Annette in 1969. They have two sons, Darren and Wayne. At school Terry played rugby alongside two great Welsh internationals, Phil Bennett and Derek Quinnell. Who knows, had he not turned to snooker as a teenager he could well have worn the famous red shirt of Wales.

Terry's son Wayne is following in dad's footsteps and turning out to be a useful snooker player. In 1987 he won the Llanelli and District Championship, the same event Terry won when he was 16 .... Wayne was only 15. There will be plenty of chance for Wayne to get as much practice in as he wants, because Terry opened his own 15-table Snooker Centre in Llanelli in 1987.

'When I play brilliant snooker I always come up against someone playing even better.'

Terry's comments after losing to Dennis Taylor in the 1987 Dulux

'At least I'm lucky, the other spectators had to pay to get in. I didn't.'

After potting only two balls in losing the first four frames to Steve Davis in the 1986 Matchroom Trophy

MIKE HALLETT

Born: 6 July 1959, Grimsby, Lincolnshire, England

Turned professional: 1979

First ranking points: 1983 Professional Players Tournament

CAREER HIGHLIGHTS

1975
National Under-16 Champion

1987
Fosters World Doubles Champion (with Stephen Hendry)

1988
Benson & Hedges Masters (runner-up)
MIM Britannia British Open (runner-up)

Rankings
1983	32
1984	25
1985	28
1986	27
1987	16
1988	9

After five years of consistent snooker, Mike Hallett made the big breakthrough he had always been threatening in 1987 when he crept into the all-important top 16 in the rankings. A 13-9 win over Silvino Francisco in the second round at the Crucible earned Mike the extra ranking point needed to push him among snooker's elite. Alex Higgins once said that Mike was 'possibly too nice' to be a top player. But in 1987 he showed a determination and character of which Alex himself would have been proud.

A nice touch which the B & SCC respect

Mike showed outstanding talent as a youngster and was the 1975 Under-16 Champion, and at the age of 19 he captained England in the Home International Championship. Mike's first job was as a shipping clerk, but snooker was his first love and he wanted to become a professional. In 1979 he applied to the WPBSA for professional status and nobody was more surprised, or delighted, than Mike himself when he was accepted. On leaving the amateur game he wrote a letter to the Billiards and Snooker Control Council thanking them for all their help given during his days before turning professional. He remains one of a small number of professionals to have made such a gesture, one that the B & SCC appreciate.

A great fan of Grand Prix motor racing, Mike was a steady but struggling middle-order professional in his first few years, but in 1983 he hit the headlines by beating Steve Davis 5-2 in the second round of the Professional Players Tournament at Bristol's Redwood Lodge. On that occasion Mike potted brilliantly and that has been an outstanding feature of his game ever since. Subsequent wins over Dennis Taylor in the 1984 Lada Classic and Alex Higgins in the same year's Rothmans did nothing but boost Mike's confidence, and confirm what a good player he is.

Hallett came close to winning a major title in 1986 when he beat Tony Knowles and Joe Johnson to reach the semi-final of the Tolly Cobbold English Professional Championship at Ipswich. In a great match against Neal Foulds, Mike was on the losing end of the 17-frame match that went its full distance.

With confidence sky high, Hallett feared no man and he showed no signs of nerves in beating the defending champion Dennis Taylor at the first hurdle at the Crucible later in the year. The man who was to succeed Taylor as champion, Joe Johnson, ended Mike's confident run with a 13-6 win.

Mike Hallett with his stable-mate Stephen Hendry in the background. The two men contested the 1988 MIM Britannia British Open at Derby; Hendry won 13–2

Mike has reached every year since 1982, he beat Tony Knowles 10-6 in the first round and then assured himself of a top-16 ranking place for 1987-88 by beating Silvino Francisco, before Neal Foulds spoilt his run in the quarter-final.

Teams up with Hendry again

Shortly after the championship Mike parted company with his manager Peter Mellor and teamed up with Stephen Hendry under Ian Doyle, signing a five-year contract. And in Australia for the Winfield Australian Masters during the summer it was Doyle's two men who contested the final, which Hendry managed to win.

Back in England, unlike the previous season, Mike started the 1987-88 season in great style. It was back to Trentham Gardens for the Fidelity Trusts International (which had superseded the BCE) but this time there were no first-round knock-outs for Mike as he produced his best result as a professional, reaching the semi-finals of a first ranking event.

In the World Doubles championship, he and Hendry came from 5-0 down to beat Dennis Taylor and Cliff Thorburn 12-8. At the start of 1988 Mike reached his first major final after wins over Dennis Taylor, Alex Higgins and John Parrott in the Benson & Hedges Masters. But in the final he suffered a 9-0 whitewash by the 'Master', Steve Davis. In the next ranking tournament he was beaten 13-2 by Stephen Hendry in the MIM Britannia British Open final.

Capable of beating the best

Mike entered 1986-87 knowing he was capable of living with, and beating, the best players in the world. After all, he had, at some time or other, beaten them. Strangely, the season started off disastrously when he lost in the first round of the BCE International at Trentham Gardens. That turned out to be the only ranking tournament in which he failed to pick up a point. Thereafter points came in all the other ranking tournaments as his meteoric rise up the rankings became all too apparent.

One of his finest moments of the season came at Northampton in

One of snooker's most improved players in 1987-8, Humberside's Mike Hallett. He reached two major finals, but lost both

December. It was not in an individual event but in the Hofmeister World Doubles when he teamed up with Stephen Hendry. They caused quite a stir by beating such notable duos as Thorburn and Thorne, Parrott and Foulds and Virgo and Stevens to reach the final. But when it comes to pairs play there is no more formidable duo than Steve Davis and Tony Meo, and the two Londoners won the title for the fourth time.

Back at the Crucible, which

> **'I'm becoming a dangerous player rather than one to make up the numbers.'**
>
> *After beating Silvino Francisco at the Crucible in 1987 Mike's re-assessment of his standing in the professional game*
>
> **'I always seem to do well in non-ranking tournaments.'**
>
> *Mike reflecting on reaching the 1986 World Doubles final . . . with no ranking points at stake!*

BARRY HEARN

Born: 1949, Dagenham, Essex, England

Somebody once described Barry Hearn as a 'streetwise chartered accountant'. That description just about sums up Hearn.

Born in Dagenham, not far from his current Romford base, Barry left school with seven O-levels and two A-levels and qualified as a chartered accountant in 1970. As for 'streetwise', there is very little Hearn doesn't know about the marketing, management and promotional side of snooker . . . and most other things for that matter.

In walks Steve Davis

His involvement with snooker started in 1974 when his company, Kendall House Investments, purchased 17 Lucania snooker halls. Barry was based at the Romford centre and his first 'managerial' involvement was with two local players, Vic Harris and Geoff Foulds. But in 1976 Barry Hearn's life changed dramatically when a young ginger-haired lad walked into the centre. That lad, of course, was Steve Davis.

Vic Harris predicted Davis would be world champion one day and Hearn was certainly impressed with what he saw and a management contract was drawn up between the two. The rest is legend. Lucania was sold in 1982 but Hearn kept possession of the Romford base and renamed it the Romford Snooker Centre, setting up his Matchroom organisation.

In early 1988 Hearn had eight players in his organisation. Tony Meo followed Davis, and Terry Griffiths became the third member of the team. Since then Dennis Taylor, Willie Thorne, Neal Foulds, Jimmy White and Cliff Thorburn have joined the camp to make Hearn the manager of the strongest team of professionals in the country. In the 1986-87 season his then seven charges scooped 45 per cent of all prize-money.

A very shrewd businessman, Hearn has arranged lucrative business deals for his players. He has also been responsible for taking the professional game abroad and into countries like China, Brazil, Hong Kong and so on. And in 1987 he launched his World Series, a world-wide contest designed to give fans in all corners of the globe the chance to see the best players in the world.

The Matchroom team is a closely knit family and Hearn regards his back room staff as important as the seven players in the limelight. One member of staff all the players rely upon is the team's chauffeur/minder: 'Robbo' Brazier.

After snooker it's boxing for Hearn

Barry took his promotional skills into the boxing world in 1987 when, after promoting his first bout at Southend, he was responsible for getting Joe Bugner to return to Britain and fight Frank

Right: Snooker's top manager Barry Hearn. Seen here holding a cue, he is a keen player and capable of knocking in regular 40–50 breaks

Below: Hearn's 'Magnificent Seven', Canada's Cliff Thorburn was added to the team in 1988

Bruno at White Hart Lane. Marathon running is another sporting activity close to Barry's heart. He has run in the London Marathon.

But snooker remains Barry's first love and he wants to see his men remain at the top of the snooker ladder for a long time to come. When Terry Wogan once asked Barry about the power struggle in snooker Hearn said: 'Power struggle? It's been and gone. We won it.'

'For someone who spends his life screwing other people, this has been a bad week for me!'

When Hearn took one leg of his World Series to Hong Kong in 1987 the owners of the venue, the Queen Elizabeth Stadium, kept finding ways of charging Hearn more money as the week went on

---

STEPHEN HENDRY

Born: 13 January 1969, Edinburgh, Scotland

Turned professional: 1985

First ranking points: 1986 Mercantile Credit Classic

Since 1985 the talk of the snooker world has revolved around Stephen Hendry. And why shouldn't it? He is, after all, the hottest property to come into the game since Jimmy White.

People in the know had been watching the progress of this enormously talented youngster long before he turned professional in 1985. The National Under-16 Champion in 1983, he went on to become the youngest winner of the Scottish Amateur title the following year when only 15. And in the World Amateur Championship at Dublin later in the year he became the tournament's youngest ever competitor.

The game's youngest professional

Hendry retained the Scottish title the following year and when he turned professional a few months later he was, at 16, the youngest player to join the professional ranks, succeeding Paddy Browne. Those who remember seeing Stephen on 'Junior Pot Black' in 1983 will remember the sight of the diminutive youngster barely tall enough to see over the top of the table. But those who did see him will have a lasting memory of a great natural talent. He has, of course, since then sprung up and no longer has problems seeing over the table.

Stephen started playing snooker on a 6-foot table when he was 12 and was an all-round sportsman at school. When he was 14 his snooker was *marginally* better than his golf, soccer and cricket.

Hendry goes limited

He was originally managed by Ron Clover, the man who once managed darts player Jockey Wilson, but Ian Doyle and Jim Marley then took the youngster under their wing and had the sense to form a limited company, Stephen Hendry Limited. They knew immediately what an investment Stephen was, and their confidence is now being justified.

When he turned professional the management team arranged a three-year cue deal with Rileys

One from the Hendry family album. Steve with mum Irene, dad Gordon and younger brother Keith. The support of his family has helped Stephen on the road to success

which could net the youngster off-the-table-earnings of around £300,000. Rileys had the same confidence in the 18-year-old as Doyle and Marley had.

After a nervous start in the professional game Stephen shone in the 1986 Mercantile Credit Classic and beat Silvino Francisco on his way to collecting his first ranking point. Neal Foulds stopped the youngster in the next round but not until Hendry had taken him to 5-4.

Hendry became the youngest winner of a national professional title when, at 17, he beat Matt Gibson for the Scottish title. He then went on to collect a second ranking point for getting to the Crucible where he pushed the more experienced Willie Thorne extremely hard before losing the match 10-8.

En route to Sheffield Stephen compiled a break of 141, which was the highest break of the championship.

A real threat to Davis

Stephen Hendry had completed his professional snooker apprenticeship. It took only 12 months. For some players it lasts a career, but he was ready to show what he was really capable of doing within a year. The 1986-87 season saw Hendry emerge as a very real prospect to succeed Steve Davis. Others had threatened before, but had fallen at the last fence – Tony Knowles, Jimmy White and Neal Foulds. They were all hailed as 'the next Steve Davis'. But in Hendry that claim looks more plausible.

Stephen gained the notable scalp of John Parrott in the 1986 BCE International and followed that with a quarter-final appearance in the Rothmans Grand Prix, where Jimmy White, the man Stephen

'Spike' after winning his first ranking tournament, the 1987 Rothmans Grand Prix at the Hexagon Theatre, Reading

'I'm going to leave school at 16 and become the youngest pro.'

. . . he did!

After Steve Davis beat Hendry in the 1987 Mercantile Davis said

'I think he'll be a top ten player in two years.'

. . . he was!

After watching the way Steve Davis helped destroy Hendry and partner Mike Hallett in the 1986 Hofmeister, Stephen reflected

'The way Steve played is what I have to set my standards to."

. . . he has!

has been likened to, scraped home 5-4. Hendry went one better in the Mercantile and reached the semi-final after whitewashing Silvino Francisco 5-0 in the quarter-final. Hendry's opponent in the semi was

CAREER HIGHLIGHTS

1983
National Under-16 Champion

1984-5
Scottish Amateur Champion

1986
Scottish Professional Champion

1987
Scottish Professional Champion
Winfield Australian Masters Champion
Rothmans Grand Prix
Fosters World Doubles Champion (with Mike Hallett)

1988
MIM Britannia British Open Champion

Rankings
1986	51
1987	23
1988	4

Emotionless when he is playing, Scotland's outstanding youngster has the same desire as Steve Davis . . . to win and not come second

Steve Davis and it was a real test of his ability. Davis turned on the pressure and was too good for the Scot and ran out the 9-3 winner.

In between those two events Hendry and his partner Mike Hallett defied their odds of 100-1 to reach the final of the Hofmeister World Doubles, only to lose to the defending champions Tony Meo and Steve Davis.

Stephen successfully retained his Scottish Professional Championship before heading for the Crucible once more in 1987. This time he turned the tables on Willie Thorne in the first round with a 10-7 win and then beat Lancashire's Steve Longworth 13-7. He was then involved in an epic battle with the defending champion Joe Johnson. Hendry was all but 'dead' at the end of the first session when 7-1 down, but he came back before losing in the 25th and last frame.

His 'youngest' records

Age	
15	Youngest winner of a national title – Scottish Amateur (1984)
15	Youngest entrant in World Amateur Championship (1984)
16	Youngest professional (1985)
17	Youngest winner of a professional event – Scottish Professional Championship (1986)
18	Youngest winner of a ranking tournament – Rothmans Grand Prix (1987)

Youngest champion

Stephen headed for Australia in the summer and became the youngest winner of a major professional title when he won the Winfield Australian Masters. On his return he added to his amazing record of being the 'youngest' winner of this-that-and-the-other when he won the Rothmans Grand Prix. In becoming the youngest winner of a ranking tournament he got the better of Steve Davis at last, winning their last-16 match 5-2. Tony Knowles, John Parrott and Dennis Taylor all fell before he lifted the trophy which elevated him into the top five of the rankings. He was the first Scot since

Walter Donaldson to lift a major championship.

He and Mike Hallett won the World Doubles title, beating Dennis Taylor and Cliff Thorburn in the final, and he beat Hallett in the MIM Britannia British Open Championship. He was one of the favourites in the 1988 World Championship, but was beaten by Jimmy White 13-12 in a brilliant

---

'He's a better player than I was at his age.'

Alex Higgins after he had beaten Hendry 9-8 in the 1986 Tennents UK Open

---

second-round match. He has two more chances to become the youngest world champion.

A superb potter, it did not take Stephen long to realise the importance of safety play. That aspect of his game now matches his potting.

He was the WPBSA Young Player of the Year in 1986 and 1987.

The trappings of success have been great. Stephen allows himself the luxury of an £18,000 Mercedes, and has invested in two houses for his mum and dad, Irene and Gordon. Apart from winning the world title Stephen's other ambition is to retire a millionaire at the age of 27.

When he first appeared on Junior Pot Black *Stephen Hendry could barely see above the table . . . but my, how he has grown since then. He's become the biggest threat to Steve Davis as the game's number one player*

ALEX HIGGINS

Born: 18 March 1949, Belfast, Northern Ireland

Turned professional: 1971

First ranking points: 1974 World Professional Championship

Alex Higgins has not won a major individual title since 1983, yet remarkably he is still among the world's top players, and when it comes down to popularity, he still has the drawing power to fill any venue. Like his fellow Ulsterman from the soccer world, George Best, Alex is brilliant but also controversial. Brushes with authority followed both men around during their tempestuous careers. But both have something else in common, the ability to draw fans.

So nearly a jockey instead

Alex, the self-styled 'people's champion', was brought up in Belfast. He started playing snooker at the age of 11 and the Jampot Club was his favourite haunt. But if he'd had his way Alex would have been a jockey and not a snooker player. When he was 14 the 7½-stone youngster left Belfast and headed for England where he was offered the chance to work as an apprentice for stable owner Eddie Reavey. But a dramatic increase in weight led to him being released without having a ride in public.

He stayed in England for a while and got a job in a paper mill and started playing snooker again. But it was then back to Belfast and the Jampot for the youngster, and he settled down to improving his game. He played for the City YMCA Club in the Belfast and District League and in 1965 he compiled his first maximum. Three years later Higgins was the Northern Ireland and All-Ireland Amateur Champion.

Alex decided it was time to make money out of the game. He turned professional in 1971 and moved to the hot-bed of northern snooker, Manchester, where he played in clubs like Potters at Salford, where many of today's professionals had an introduction to money-match snooker.

A win that changed the course of snooker

Within a year of turning professional Higgins was the champion of the world and his victory changed the face of British snooker. His arrival generated much needed publicity for the sport. The World Championship was the first snooker event to receive daily coverage in the press for more than ten years. Just like Tony Jacklin when he won the Open golf championship in 1969, Higgins' win was an inspiration to the ordinary man-in-the-street to go out and emulate him. He made the game look simple.

One of the game's most controversial characters, Alex Higgins. Despite his outbursts, he has been good for the game since becoming the youngest world champion in 1972

CAREER HIGHLIGHTS

1968
Northern Ireland Amateur Champion

1972
World Professional Champion

1978
Benson & Hedges Masters Champion

1980
British Gold Cup Champion

1981
Benson & Hedges Masters Champion

1982
Embassy World Professional Champion

1983
Irish Professional Champion
Coral UK Champion

1984
Hofmeister World Doubles Champion (with Jimmy White)

1985
World Cup (member of winning All-Ireland team)

1986
World Cup (member of winning Ireland 'A' team)

1987
World Cup (member of winning Ireland 'A' team)

Rankings

Year	Rank
1983	5
1984	9
1985	9
1986	6
1987	9
1988	17

His World Championship success was at the Selly Oak British Legion in Birmingham, and was a far cry from the plush surroundings of the Crucible Theatre. Planks of wood on beer crates helped make up the tiered seating, but the atmosphere was provided by Alex.

Higgins had beaten three giants of the game in Jackie Rea, John Pulman and Rex Williams (31-30) to reach the final at the first attempt. And the man standing between Higgins and an historic win was John Spencer, the reigning champion. But Higgins went on to win 37-32 and became the youngest winner of the title. He still holds that honour today, although the distinction is being constantly threatened by the ever-increasing number of youngsters coming into the professional game. For winning the title in 1972 Alex collected a cheque for just £480 . . . His unique style added a new dimension to the game and his exciting play helped popularise snooker.

When his game is 'on song' Alex Higgins is one of the most exciting players in the world to watch

'You know my trouble, I've been drinking too much water.'

Once, when having a bad spell, he blamed it on drinking too much water . . . he did have a preference for lager and vodka at the time

A T-shirt seen during the 1983 World Championship at Sheffield bore the following print

'On the 8th day God created Alex Higgins.'

Alex was to suffer the disappointment of losing two world championship finals, to Ray Reardon in 1976, and to Cliff Thorburn, in an epic battle which the Canadian won 18-16, in 1980. But in 1982, and ten years after his first success, Alex Higgins became World Champion for the second time.

Getting to the final had been a long hard battle for Alex. He beat Doug Mountjoy 13-12, Willie Thorne 13-10 and in the semi-final had a momentous 16-15 win over Jimmy White, after being two down with three frames to play. In the final Alex had it no easier and was locked at 15-all with the former champion Ray Reardon, before the Welshman made two mistakes to let Alex pull away to 17-15. Alex sewed the match up in the next frame with a 135 clearance. Millions watching on television will never forget the scenes at the end when a tearful Alex called wife Lynn and daughter Lauren into the arena to share his moment of triumph. Sadly, there has been little for Alex to celebrate since then, and the marriage to Lynn has ended.

The Higgins-Davis rivalry begins

The rivalry between Alex and Steve Davis is well documented and it all started in 1980 when Higgins won their first meeting in the quarter-final of the Embassy World Championship. However, Davis started to dominate their meetings, but in 1983 Alex went

---

Tony Francis once said about Alex

'Higgins treats his talent like a mistress; he flirts with it, neglects it, and then expects it to come running back when he snaps his fingers . . .'

A poll at the London Dungeon Museum in 1986 was taken to see whom visitors would most like to see in stocks and pelted with eggs and rotten vegetables. Poor Alex could only come third behind Dirty Den and Sid the mystery gas-advert man

---

His rivalry with Steve Davis

Alex Higgins beat Steve Davis the first time they met, in the 1980 World Championship. By early 1988 they had met in ten more ranking events and Davis has won all of them. The full list of meetings in ranking events is:

1980 Embassy World Championship	Quarter-final	9-13
1981 Embassy World Championship	Second round	13-8
1983 Embassy World Championship	Semi-final	16-5
1984 Jameson International	Quarter-final	5-1
1984 Coral UK Open	Final	16-8
1985 Mercantile Credit Classic	Second round	5-2
1985 Rothmans Grand Prix	Fifth round	5-0
1986 Dulux British Open	Semi-final	9-3
1986 Tennents UK Open	Semi-final	9-3
1987 Tennents UK Open	Fifth round	9-2
1988 Mercantile Credit Classic	Fifth round	5-0

Higgins' record is:

Frames
For   Against
37   101

---

part of the way to gaining retribution by winning the Coral 16-15 in one of the game's greatest matches. Trailing 7-0 at the end of the first session, Alex started clawing his way back before eventually winning in the 31st and last frame. By mid 1988 the two men had met 21 times and Alex had only won four times, as above and in the non-ranking Masters and Irish Masters.

That Coral UK Championship success was Alex's last win in an individual open competition, although he did team up with Jimmy White to dethrone Davis and Tony Meo as World Doubles Champions in 1984. He has also been a member of the All-Ireland team that won the World Cup three times between 1985 and 1987.

Countless managers

Alex has had many managers over the years. There was the former bingo entrepreneur John McLoughlin, who now runs a snooker club in Blackburn. Then Dennis Broderick had a spell as Alex's manager. The West End promotions company of West Nally (the West being commentator Peter West) looked after Alex for a while. Then Maurice Hayes of Q Promotions had a stint. Geoff

Lomas (Alex's best man when he married Lynn in 1980) also had a spell, and so did Del Simmons. Simmons was the man who, almost every time his name appeared in print, was neither prefixed or suffixed with 'the WPBSA's £65,000-a-year contracts negotiator'.

A Mr D. Wigglesworth of Pontefract, West Yorkshire, wrote to Snooker Scene *in 1982 and said*

'I am writing to ask why every time Alex Higgins makes a foul he wants the rules changing?'

When Dennis Taylor fluked a red after Alex played a safety shot during their match in the 1982 Yamaha Organs Trophy Alex said to Taylor after he had 'stolen' the frame and the match

'Don't ever speak to me again. Don't speak to my wife or daughter. And don't speak to my cat!'

'That's a tough one. Give me a year to think about it.'

When someone close to Alex was asked what he was really like that was the answer . . .

Harvey Lisberg of Sportsworld next had the responsibility of looking after Alex before the 'WPBSA's £65,000-a-year contracts negotiator' had another spell. Alex then teamed up with pop music magnate Howard Kruger in 1986 and joined his Framework team.

Skirmishes with authorities have formed part of Alex's story for most of his snooker life. Brushes with WPBSA officials and the 'watering' of a BBC flower arrangement have done little to enhance his image. But they have done little to harm his popularity. Alex is a great individualist and nobody should ever try to take that away from him. Take that away and you may as well take Alex Higgins away. Love him or hate him, there is no doubting that Alex Higgins is one of the most naturally talented players ever to pick up a cue.

The self-styled 'people's champion' seems to be bored . . . He's not really, he's just having a few problems getting his bow tie off – it is one of the first things Alex does, when he enters the arena, because he hates the restriction of a tie

EUGENE HUGHES

Born: 4 November 1955, Dun Laoghaire, County Dublin, Republic of Ireland

Turned professional: 1981

First ranking points: 1983 Professional Players Tournament

Irishman Eugene Hughes

Since he turned professional in 1981 Eugene Hughes has consistently remained in the world's top 35. Today, as the number of professionals has reached 128, he is regularly 'knocking on the door' of the big championships.

Hughes started playing snooker at the Monkstown WMC when he was 15 and he went on to become one of the game's top amateur players in the 1970s. He won the billiards and snooker National Under-19 titles in 1975 and then went on to win four Republic of Ireland Amateur titles at both games. He represented his country in the Home International Championships and in the 1980 Amateur World Championship in Australia he compiled a championship record break of 128 which stood until bettered by Malta's Tony Drago four years later.

Eugene first came to London in 1977-78 and was based at the Pot Black Club in Clapham, but did not like the city lights and returned home. When he turned professional in 1981 he was back in England but based in Loughborough. After a succession of disappointments Eugene reached the Crucible stage of the World Championship in 1983 but lost 10-7 to the former champion Ray Reardon in the first round. He started the next season by beating Bill Werbeniuk and Terry Griffiths to reach the quarter-final of the Professional Players Tournament at Redwood Lodge.

He started the 1984-85 season by reaching the semi-final of the Jameson International. Victories over Doug Mountjoy, Ray Reardon and a revenge win over Thorne put Hughes into a semi-final clash with Steve Davis. He collected £10,000 as the losing semi-finalist as Davis ran out the comfortable 9-3 winner.

Apart from reaching the quarter-final of the Dulux British Open where he lost to fellow Irishman Alex Higgins, the 1984-85 season had little to offer by way of individual glories for Hughes but he was a member of the All-Ireland team that won the World Cup event.

Eugene moved from Ireland and became the resident professional at the Kings Cross Snooker Centre. Having a base in England helped improve Eugene's game and in 1986 he reached the last 16 of the World Championship at Sheffield before losing to Cliff Thorburn. Again, he teamed up with Higgins and Taylor to retain the World Cup for Ireland.

Steve Davis . . . the biggest scalp of his career

Having become the resident professional at the Ilford Snooker Centre in the summer Eugene beat a succession of lower ranked players before meeting Steve Davis in the last eight of the season's first ranking event, the BCE International at Stoke-on-Trent's Trentham Gardens. Davis had won all three of their previous meetings but Hughes upset the odds when he beat the World Champion 5-4. Davis' stablemate Neal Foulds ended Eugene's ambitions of a first major final 9-8 in their semi-final.

Later he lost 10-9 to defending champion Joe Johnson at the Crucible. Hughes' game received a lift when he joined Howard Kruger's Framework team. A slow, deliberate player, his main aim is to get into the top 16 in the world. He has hovered in the low 20s.

CAREER HIGHLIGHTS

1975
National Under-19 Billiards and Snooker Champion

1977
Republic of Ireland Amateur Billiards Champion

1978
Republic of Ireland Amateur Billiards and Snooker Champion

1979
Republic of Ireland Amateur Snooker Champion
All-Ireland Amateur Snooker Champion

1984
Jameson International (semi-final)

1985
World Cup (member of winning All-Ireland team)

1986
BCE International (semi-final)
World Cup (member of winning Ireland 'A' team)

1987
World Cup (member of winning Ireland 'A' team)

Rankings
1983	35
1984	27
1985	21
1986	20
1987	24
1988	21

STEVE JAMES

Born: 2 May 1961, Cannock, Staffordshire, England

Turned professional: 1986

First ranking point: 1987 Dulux British Open

CAREER HIGHLIGHTS

1988
Embassy World Professional Championship (quarter-final)

Ranking
1987   67
1988   32

Steve James was one of eight new professionals in 1986 as a result of coming through the first of the Professional Ticket Tournaments the previous year. A former member of the Wednesbury Conservative Club in the West Midlands League, he was a team-mate of current professionals Martin Clark, Anthony Harris and Jim Chambers.

He had an encouraging debut season as a professional and reached the last 16 of the Tolly Ales English Professional Championship. Although world champion Joe Johnson ended his hopes at that stage, Steve had beaten John Hargreaves, Fred Davis and Steve Longworth to get to the final phase.

That achievement was immediately followed by a good run in the Dulux British Open that earned him his first ranking point but Rex Williams deprived Steve

of his television debut by winning 5–2 in the fourth round.

Steve ended his first season ranked number 67 but he improved on that considerably in 1987-8 thanks to reaching the last 16 of the first ranking event of the season, the Fidelity Unit Trusts at Stoke-on-Trent.

A fine win over John Campbell in the last qualifying round set Steve up for his television debut against another man playing in front of the cameras for the first time, David Roe. James won 5–3 and earned the right to meet Cliff Thorburn in the next round, when the Canadian won.

Then he and David Roe reached the semi-final of the Fosters World Doubles championship at Northampton, despite starting the tournament as 500–1 outsiders.

Their attacking style of play brought them wins over such notable pairings as Dave Martin and

John Spencer and, in the quarter-final, over John Parrott and Dean Reynolds. They were pulled back Reynolds. But in the semi-final Cliff Thorburn and Dennis Taylor ousted them convincingly 9-1, despite the Midlanders winning the opening frame. The highlight of Steve's career came in the 1988 World Professional Championship, where he beat Rex Williams and former champion Joe Johnson before losing 13-11 to Cliff Thorburn in the quarter-final. Furthermore, in the first round he made a break of 140, which took the highest break prize of £9,500, by far his best pay day so far.

Steve James, one of the UK's promising young players

JOE JOHNSON

Born: 29 July 1952, Bradford, Yorkshire, England

Turned professional: 1979

First ranking points: 1982 Professional Players Tournament

After the appalling tragedy of the Bradford Football Club fire disaster in 1985 it was justice that the city should have some cause to celebrate. Six days before the first anniversary of the disaster Bradford's favourite son Joe Johnson became snooker champion of the world. On that day Joe not only won the trophy for himself and his wife Terryl and their six children; he won it for the city he loves so dearly, Bradford.

Grossly underrated for many years, Joe was a good working professional and very popular with players and fans alike. There was not a fellow professional who begrudged him victory over Steve Davis at the Crucible in 1986 — except Steve that is!

Television problem for many years

Joe had the big problems of being unable to produce results in front of the television cameras. It appeared that he had a mental blockage when on TV, but the reality is he found it difficult to adjust to the lights. Joe held the world record break by an amateur when he made a 140 break at the Middlesbrough TUC club in 1978. Ironically the break was covered by Tyne Tees Television!

When Joe reached his first major professional final, the 1983 Professional Players Tournament at Bristol, he beat Jimmy White, Eddie Charlton, Cliff Thorburn and Tony Meo before putting up a great fight in going down 9-8 to Tony Knowles. The tournament was untelevised and seemed to bear out Joe's preference for playing without the cameras. It was only when Joe beat Welshman Cliff Wilson in the second round of the 1985 Mercantile that he overcame his 'handicap' and won a match for the first time in four attempts on television.

After beating Wilson, Joe went on to beat Warren King before losing to Cliff Thorburn in the semi-finals, but that performance helped Joe climb into the world top 16 at the end of the season.

Morley snooker centre . . . Joe's second home

A very good amateur, Johnson was the National Under-19 Champion in 1971. He was three times Yorkshire Champion and in 1978 lost to Terry Griffiths in the final of the English Amateur Championship. He also lost to Cliff Wilson in the final of that year's World Amateur Championship in Malta. Joe turned professional in 1979 and while he enjoyed a profitable time playing the pro-am circuit, he just couldn't make the breakthrough on the professional circuit until that 1983 Professional Players Tournament. The year before Joe had become the resident professional at the Morley Snooker Centre, which employed him on the advice of Yorkshire's senior player, John Dunning. Joe still has an affection for the club and it was the first place he went on his return from winning the world title at Sheffield in 1986.

150-1 outsider

Joe did not make his Crucible debut until 1984 and it was an occasion he would be only too pleased to forget, because he lost 10-1 to Dennis Taylor. The following year he lost in the first round to Canadian Bill Werbeniuk. So when he arrived in 1986 it was hardly surprising he was 150-1 to win the title. But those odds counted for nothing as he beat Dave Martin and Mike Hallett before his biggest test, a

Top: Joe Johnson with wife Terryl after his great victory over Steve Davis in the 1986 World Championship at Sheffield

Above: One of the game's most down to earth players, Joe loves returning to his native Bradford

the year to repay them for their support. He neglected the one thing vital to keep you at the top, and that was practice. His appetite for the game went for a while but when he returned to the Crucible a year later he came with a mission, to retain the title.

Joe was asked shortly after winning the world title: 'When will you feel the pressure of being world champion?' His reply

'When I've lost in the first round next year.'

. . . but he didn't

Repeat final

Joe nervously overcame Eugene Hughes in the first round, won comfortably over Murdo McLeod in the next and then beat Scot Stephen Hendry in a great quarter-final. In the semi-final Neal Foulds started favourite but was no match for Joe and so a repeat of the 1986 final was set up, the first such repeat at the Crucible. This time Davis gained his revenge with an 18-14 win, but just reaching the final was a great boost to Joe's morale. Had he won, goodness knows what *that* would have done.

He went on to win the first tournament of the 1987-88 British season, the Langs Scottish Masters and reached the semi-final of the Tennents UK Championship after a heart attack scare.

A former apprentice motor mechanic, transport office worker and pipe layer with the Gas Board, Joe has remained a down-to-earth Yorkshire lad and is not one for the fame and glory. During his World Championship winning year he preferred a drink with the lads after each match in the public bar, and not in the hospitality lounge.

Joe also gets as much pleasure out of singing as he does playing snooker and he has been seen fronting with the Preston band 'Made in Japan'.

CAREER HIGHLIGHTS

1971
National Under-19 Champion

1978
World Amateur Championship (runner-up)

1986
Embassy World Professional Champion

1987
Embassy World Professional Championship (runner-up) Langs Scottish Masters Champion

Rankings

Year	Rank
1983	23
1984	19
1985	16
1986	8
1987	5
1988	11

---

quarter-final meeting with Terry Griffiths. Johnson won a great encounter 13-12 and by comparison his semi-final win over Tony Knowles was an easy affair.

The crowd warmed to him and when he lined up against Steve Davis they were firmly on his side, simply for the age-old reason: that British fans love the underdog. That is certainly what Joe was . . . but he didn't play like it. He approached the game with a nothing-to-lose attitude and it paid dividends. He won 18-12 and was one of the most popular champions for many years.

That win had an adverse affect on Joe. It should have spurred him to greater glories the following season but it did the opposite and he struggled for most of the season, suffering defeats by lower ranked players. In all fairness to Joe, he spent much of his year as world champion taking himself to the people who had helped him over

TONY JONES

Born: 15 April 1960, Sutton-in-Ashfield, Nottinghamshire, England

Turned professional: 1983

First ranking points: 1986 Mercantile Credit Classic

CAREER HIGHLIGHTS

1983
English Amateur Champion

1984-5
Hofmeister World Doubles
(runner-up, with Ray Reardon)

1988
MIM Britannia British Open
(last 16)

Rankings

1983	–	1986	55
1984	–	1987	46
1985	50	1988	49

Tony Jones started playing snooker seriously around the Nottingham area in 1981. Within two years he had beaten John Parrott to become the English Amateur Champion and thus have his name engraved on the famous trophy alongside the likes of Ray Reardon, John Pulman, Rex Williams, John Spencer, and more recently, Jimmy White.

Tony, who was first introduced to snooker at the age of 13 by a local deaf and dumb boy, won his first title, the Nottinghamshire Junior Championship, at 15. A complete natural, he has never been coached.

He left school at 16 and had a couple of factory jobs before moving to Chesterfield in 1981 to become the resident player/coach at the Chesterfield Snooker

Tony Jones (left) with his partner Ray Reardon, referee Len Ganley and opponents Dennis Taylor and Terry Griffiths

Centre. At the time of the 1983 English Amateur Championship Jones had 'transferred' to the Sheffield Snooker Centre, and in winning the coveted title he claimed notable scalps in Neal Foulds, in the Southern Area final, and John Parrott in the final itself.

Tony returns to Sheffield

Tony was accepted as a professional in June 1983 and joined Ron Gross in London. However, he never lived up to his early promise. An excellent potter, he worked hard at getting his safety play right and in 1985, after coming through four qualifying matches, he returned to Sheffield for his Crucible debut. In losing by only 10-8 to Tony Knowles, Jones showed in front of the television cameras how he had won the English Amateur.

Tony received a boost that year when he teamed up with Ray Reardon in the Hofmeister World Doubles and they turned out to be the surprise pairing, going all the way to the final. Reardon will be the first to admit that Tony more than 'paid his way' in getting them there. At the last hurdle the pairs specialists of Davis and Meo proved too strong for the Anglo-Welsh pairing and the former champions ran out 12-5 winners.

With the security of a sponsorship deal with Embassy Double Glazing of Chesterfield behind him Tony reached the last 16 of the MIM Britannia British Open, where he lost to Stephen Hendry, after beating Alex Higgins 5-3 in the third round.

WAYNE JONES

Born: 24 December 1959, Tredegar, Monmouthshire, Wales

Turned professional: 1984

First ranking points: 1985 Rothmans Grand Prix

CAREER HIGHLIGHTS

1983
Welsh Amateur Champion

1986
Tennents UK Open (quarter-final)

1988
Welsh Professional Championship (runner-up)

Rankings
1985	49
1986	56
1987	34
1988	34

It may not be shown in his career highlights, but one of Wayne Jones' truly great snooker moments was at the Abertysswg Working Men's Club in 1986. In practice against Reg Harvey Wayne compiled the first-ever 147 break at the famous club. In this day and age when maximums are being made with such regularity, it may not seem much of an achievement but, when you consider the Abertysswg WMC has groomed such great Welsh talents as Des May, Alwyn Lloyd and Doug Mountjoy then yes, it is a fair achievement.

Wayne had been playing at the club ever since he was nine and a half. His mother died when he was young and when his father remarried and moved away from the area Wayne stayed to be brought up by his grandfather who encouraged his snooker playing.

That encouragement was rewarded in 1983 when Wayne, a former bricklayer and landscape gardener, beat the three times champion Terry Parsons to win the Welsh Amateur crown. That win was fully justified as Jones spent at least 4-5 hours a day practising, either at the one table of the Abertysswg club, or at the Scala in Merthyr.

1986, a good snooker year
Wayne's first year as a professional saw him reach the last 32 of the Jameson International and then reach the Crucible, where he lost 10-4 to Jimmy White.

When reaching the quarter-final of the Tennents in 1986 Wayne was asked what he put his change of fortunes down to. His answer was

'Fifteen years of hard practice.'

Wayne Jones enjoyed a great win over Ray Reardon to reach the semi-final of the Welsh Professional Championship in 1986.

In the next ranking tournament, the Tennents UK Open, Wayne was spurred to his greatest performance as a professional in beating Dennis Taylor and Eugene Hughes (against whom he made his maiden television century, 106) before meeting another Irishman, Alex Higgins. Higgins won their quarter-final encounter 9-5 but that was the springboard Jones needed and he went to the last 16 of the next event, the Mercantile Credit Classic, before being ousted by fellow Welshman Cliff Wilson but that was after he had achieved his second win over Dennis Taylor in a week.

He beat Doug Mountjoy in the semi-final of the 1988 Welsh Professional championship before losing to Terry Griffiths in the final.

Runner-up in the Welsh Professional Championship in 1988, Wayne Jones is now a threat to Wales' 'big three'

WARREN KING

Born: 1 April 1955, Sydney, Australia

Turned professional: 1982

First ranking points: 1985 Mercantile Credit Classic

The reign of Eddie Charlton as Australia's top player came to an end in 1985 when John Campbell broke his 20-year domination of the Australian Professional Championship. Since then, however, the next in the line of top Australians has emerged in the form of Warren King.

A former New South Wales Champion, King won the Australian amateur title in 1980 and 1981 and since 1985 he has twice won the professional title. Unlike Charlton, who spent many of his formative professional years in Britain, King can rightly claim to be the best home-produced professional since Warren Simpson more than 20 years ago.

He started playing snooker at Sydney's Granville Sports Club at the age of 15. The biggest influence on his career was his mother Sue, who funded his games.

World Cup stardom

King first attracted attention in Britain when, as a member of Australia's World Cup team in 1983, he beat Cliff Thorburn 2-1 and took a frame off Kirk Stevens to prove he could compete against the best players on the circuit, and under pressure.

In individual events Warren had his greatest moment at the beginning of 1985 when he reached the quarter-final of the Mercantile Credit Classic. Successive breaks of 94 and 80 saw him beat Jimmy White on the way and in the quarter-final he led Joe Johnson 3-2 before losing 5-3.

The experience Warren gained in Britain paid dividends when he returned to Australia. In winning his first Australian professional title he showed maturity in beating the defending champion John Campbell 10-3 in the final at Wool-

Warren King eyes up a shot

longong near Sydney. His 111 clearance against Charlton in the semi-final was the only century of the competition.

Warren retained his title the following year when he beat Charlton 10-7 in a marathon contest. King's 120 break in the final was, once more, the highest of the tournament.

Davis and Foulds . . . nearly two great wins

King's best season to date has been 1986-87. He started by collecting a ranking point in the season's first tournament, the BCE International, when he reached the fourth round. He lost to Steve Davis, but not until he had caused a sensation by pulling Davis back from 1-4 to level it at 4-all, before Davis won the deciding frame.

A couple of months later he came close to pulling off the best result of his career when he led Neal Foulds 4-1 in the best-of-nine frame fourth-round match in the Dulux British Open. Foulds pulled one back and the seventh frame went to a respotted black. King missed the pot by a fraction

of an inch. Foulds won that frame and went on to win the match 5-4. King's talent was not going unnoticed and he received further rave notices in the World Championship at Sheffield.

It was the second time he had reached the Crucible. On the other occasion, in 1984 Steve Davis beat him 10-3. Now, three years later, Warren had the chance to put the record straight as the pair of them were pitched into battle in the first round. Davis suspected he had a match on his hands after King had beaten Eddie Charlton 10-4 in a qualifying round, and his suspicions were well founded. The former champion raced to a 7-2 interval lead and then led 8-3, needing just two frames for victory. King won four frames in succession to make it 8-7, and was within a ball of making it 8-all, but Davis changed gear and won the next two vital frames to clinch victory in one of the toughest matches in his run-up to regaining his title.

Warren, with Eddie Charlton and John Campbell, took Australia to the final of the Festina World Cup in 1988.

Now based at the Cue Ball Club in Southampton, King loves skiing, backgammon and playing cards.

CAREER HIGHLIGHTS

1980-81
Australian Amateur Champion

1985
*Mercantile Credit Classic
(quarter-final)*

1986-87
*Australian Professional
Champion*

Rankings
1983	–
1984	48
1985	35
1986	41
1987	39
1988	44

TONY KNOWLES

Born: 13 June 1955, Bolton, Lancashire, England

Turned professional: 1980

First ranking points: 1982 Embassy World Professional Championship

CAREER HIGHLIGHTS

1972 and 1974
National Under-19 Champion

1982
Jameson International Champion

1983
Embassy World Professional Championship (semi-final)
World Team Classic (member of winning England team)
Professional Players Tournament Champion

1984
Winfield Australian Masters Champion

1985
Embassy World Professional Championship (semi-final)

1986
Embassy World Professional Championship (semi-final)

Rankings

1983	4	1986	4
1984	2	1987	7
1985	3	1988	8

The glamour boy of snooker, Tony Knowles first gained national attention in 1982 when he ousted Steve Davis from the Embassy World Professional Championship. A professional of less than two years, Tony had shown he was capable of upsetting the best when he beat Doug Mountjoy to reach the quarter-final of the 1981 Coral UK Championship but there was not a person in the land who believed Knowles would beat Davis, let alone beat him 10-1. But he did.

It looked as though Tony was going to go through life labelled as 'The man who beat Steve Davis 10-1'. But at the start of the next season he won the Jameson International and the media attention was focused on 'Tony Knowles – champion'.

Top junior and top amateur

Born in Bolton, Knowles was introduced to snooker at an early age by his father, who was the steward at the Tonge Moor Conservative Club. Tony first picked up a cue at the age of nine and would spend as many hours as he could on any empty table available. After leaving school Tony went to art college but abandoned all other plans to pursue a snooker career. He showed signs that he was justified in making that decision when he won the Under-19 Championship in 1972. On the morning of the final Tony compiled his first 100 break in practice. Two years later he regained the title. Tony gained international honours in 1978 and won all four of his matches in the Home International series. The following year he won all five matches and was voted the Player of the Series.

After serving a long apprentice-ship in the amateur game Tony put in his first application for professional status in November 1979 but was rejected. However, the WPBSA accepted his second application a couple of months later.

That great Crucible run

Once the euphoria of beating Davis in the 1982 World Championship had died down Tony went on to beat Graham Miles 13-7 in the next round. Just as he was being talked about as a possible surprise champion, Eddie Charlton brought him back to earth with a narrow 13-11 quarter-final win.

At the start of the following season Davis had the chance to

Snooker's 'golden boy' of the early 1980s, Tony Knowles from Bolton

His record against Steve Davis since beating him 10-1

Since beating Davis 10-1 in the 1982 World Championship Tony Knowles has not beaten him in a major professional match. This is how he has fared since that glorious day at the Crucible:

1982	Langs Scottish Masters	First round	lost 4-5
1983	Langs Scottish Masters	Final	6-9
1984	Tolly Cobbold Classic	Final	2-8
1984	Jameson International	Final	2-9
1985	Tolly Cobbold English Professional Championship	Final	2-9

gain revenge for his 10-1 defeat when the two men were paired in the first round of the Langs Scottish Masters. Davis did get his revenge with a 5-4 win.

Tony climbed to fourth in the rankings in 1982-83 after winning the Jameson International, the first event after the World Championship to be accorded ranking status. On his way to the final, where he beat David Taylor 9-6, Tony beat Ray Reardon, Cliff Wilson and Kirk Stevens. Knowles ended the season by reaching the semi-final

Away from the snooker table Tony Knowles enjoys holidaying in the Tenerife sun at Playa de las Americas or waterskiing in the Lake District. He is also a keen horse racing owner

of the World Championship after beating Graham Miles, Ray Reardon (13-12), and Tony Meo. But Cliff Thorburn, who went on to win the title, came out on top by 16 frames to 15.

Tony moved up the rankings even further in 1983-84 when he climbed to second place – a remarkable rise in two years.

Tony's turn to feel the effect of a giant-killing act

His only win of the season was in the untelevised Professional Players Tournament at Redwood Lodge, Bristol. He won a great final 9-8 against Joe Johnson after he had seemed to be cruising to an easy win. Knowles collected more ranking points in the Lada Classic but he was then on the receiving end of a giant-killing act, when Liverpool's John Parrott emerged as a new superstar after beating him (and Alex Higgins) 5-1. Parrott also upset the odds in the first round of the Embassy when he inflicted another defeat on Tony, winning 10-7.

Tony has held on to his top 10 position since then but has dropped slightly. He has, however, attracted a lot of attention from his off-the-table activities. He was fined £5,000 by the WPBSA in 1984 following his 'tell-all' stories in the *Sun* newspaper in an act which Barry Hearn described as 'professional suicide'. Then Tony's former girl friend Suzie Harrison sold her story. It was shortly after this incident that Tony met Howard Kruger while on holiday in Marbella and Kruger

Tony Knowles first hit the headlines in the 1982 World Championship when he beat Steve Davis 10-1 but he proved that result was no fluke as he pulled himself to number two in the rankings

offered to act as Tony's manager.

Knowles has not won a major championship since the 1983 Professional Players Tournament but reached the final of the Jameson International in 1984, when Steve Davis beat him 9-2. In the follow-

---

When Tony made his first century break on the morning of the 1972 Junior Championship it was made in the dark because he didn't have enough money to put in the light meter . . .

'No matter how well you're playing you don't improve unless you play the best players."

A realistic view from Tony

---

ing season's English Professional Championship final Davis won by the same score.

Another semi-final appearance at Sheffield followed in 1985 but the eventual champion Dennis Taylor ousted Knowles 16-5. He reached the semi-final a year later but lost to the eventual winner yet again, when Joe Johnson beat him 16-8. There was no such progress in 1987 when Mike Hallett was the surprise winner of their first-round clash.

Refreshed and raring to go again

Tony spent the summer of 1987 playing tennis and water skiing, and came back to the game feeling

Tony Knowles, one of the glamour boys of snooker

refreshed. He reached the last 16 of the season's first ranking event, the Fidelity Unit Trusts International, and the last eight of the next, the Rothmans Grand Prix. He reached the semi-final of the Mercantile, where he lost to John Parrott again. Adding two inches to the middle of his cue also helped improve his game.

Knowles played well in the 1988 World Championship, reaching the quarter-final, where he met Jimmy White. At 10-2 to White the match looked over but Tony pulled back to 10-6 before White won the last three frames needed to win.

HOWARD KRUGER

Born: 1959, Brighton, Sussex, England

After meeting Tony Knowles on holiday in Marbella Howard Kruger and Knowles built up a friendship. And when Tony said he needed a business manager because of the bad press he was receiving at the time, Howard was only too pleased to assist. That was in 1986, and so was born the Framework team.

'After dealing with pop groups Alex is a saint!'

. . . I'll bet that's the first time Alex has been called a saint

'We can get round Alex's tarnished image.'

. . . so said Howard after becoming Higgins' manager in 1986

The team is increasing all the time and started the 1987-88 season with an eight-strong membership.

Tony Knowles was not, however, Kruger's first involvement in sports management. That started when he acted on behalf of the soccer player Steve Foster, and he later managed footballer Graeme Souness and swimmer Sharon Davies. He also promoted skaters Torvill and Dean for two years. He has show business running through his veins and is the chief executive of the mammoth Kruger Organisation which was founded by his father Jeffrey. They have been involved with concert promotions, videos, films, and almost everything to do with the music business. They have offices in Belgravia, Brighton, Los Angeles and New York.

Framework expands

After Tony Knowles, the next Framework recruit was Alex Higgins and for a while Kruger acted as an agent for Jimmy White. The other members of the team at the start of the 1987-88 season were John Parrott, Joe Johnson, Dean Reynolds, Martin Clark, Eugene Hughes and Mark Bennett.

Kruger and Barry Hearn have 16 of the top players between them and when Joe Johnson broke the Hearn monopoly by winning the 1987 Langs Scottish Masters Howard said: 'This is the win all the lads at Framework have been waiting for. I reckon the rest of the snooker world will also be relieved to see someone outside the Matchroom camp take a title.'

From pop music to snooker, that was the transformation made by Howard Kruger when he started the Framework team. They now offer the biggest threat en masse to Barry Hearn's Matchroom outfit

STEVE LONGWORTH

Born: 27 July 1948, Blackburn, Lancashire, England

Turned professional: 1984

First ranking points: 1985 Mercantile Credit Classic

CAREER HIGHLIGHTS

1984
English Amateur Champion

1987
Embassy World Professional Championship (last 16)

Rankings
1985	37
1986	31
1987	31
1988	30

In 1971 Steve Longworth was a member of the Benarth Club in Blackburn which won the Lancashire team title. His fellow teammates were Phil Hollings, Dennis Taylor and Jim Meadowcroft. Hollings has faded into snooker obscurity, but Taylor and Meadowcroft have certainly made a name for themselves in the snooker world.

It looked as though Steve Longworth might have gone the same way as Hollings because he packed the game in, apart from playing in local leagues, until the late 1970s when he started to re-establish himself as a leading amateur. And in 1984 the former van driver beat Wayne Jones at the Commonwealth Sporting Club at Blackpool to become the first Lancastrian since David Taylor in 1968 to win the English amateur crown.

Wife Madeline prevents an early retirement

Steve turned professional that year, having been rejected by the WPBSA two years earlier. After early defeats in his first three ranking events, Steve was all for packing up again and getting a regular job. His wife Madeline talked him out of it and in the next major event, the Mercantile, he reached the last 16 and enjoyed wins over Neal Foulds and David Taylor, before losing to Cliff Thorburn on his television debut. Longworth went on to reach the semi-final of the English Professional Championship after what Steve describes as 'The best win of my career' – the victory over Jimmy White 9-5 in the quarter-final. Fellow Lancastrian Tony Knowles beat Steve in the semi-final.

In his second season as a professional Steve broke into the all-important top 32 and has stayed there ever since. In 1987, at the third attempt, he reached the Crucible stage of the Embassy World Professional Championship. He won his debut match in snooker's 'melting pot' by beating Kirk Stevens 10-4 before losing to Scotland's Stephen Hendry.

Managed by John McLoughlin at the Centre Club in Blackburn, Steve lives in the town with his wife and two daughters. Already firmly established as one of the country's leading players, he is capable of improving on his ranking position even further.

'I've never felt pressure like it.'

Steve's comments about his Crucible debut in 1987

A former Blackburn van driver, Steve Longworth is hoping he can deliver the goods on the snooker table soon

TED LOWE

Born: 1 November 1920, Lambourn, Berkshire

Ted Lowe is the 'voice of snooker' and has held that position since standing in for Raymond Glendenning behind the microphone in September 1954. On that occasion there were no sophisticated commentary boxes with monitors and so on, and Lowe had to sit in the front row. So as not to disturb the players' concentration he was asked to whisper into the microphone. That is why today he still talks in soft tones and is nicknamed 'Whispering Ted'.

The BBC coverage on that occasion was at the famous Leicester Square Hall where Ted was the general manager, a position he had held since 1947 when the hall re-opened after a German bomb destroyed it (then known as Thurston's Hall) during the war. Ted got the job at the Leicester Square Hall when he met Joe Davis in 1945. Joe, part proprietor of the hall, was giving an exhibition at the Smith's Meters Social

All TV commentators have eligible entries for 'Colemanballs' and Ted is no exception. He once said

'The audience is standing to relieve themselves!'

. . . and on another occasion he said of referee John Smyth who was about to mark the position of the cue-ball before cleaning it

'John Smyth's getting his little implement out!'

Club where Ted was secretary. Joe asked Ted to become general manager when the club re-opened, and Ted accepted. After the hall closed in 1955 Ted worked at Allied Breweries until November 1980 when he retired.

'Pot Black' – Ted's idea

As a player Ted's best achievement was to reach the semi-final of the 1946 London section of the English Amateur Championship. But his real claim to fame is his contribution to the rebirth of snooker in the late 1960s.

In 1969 he was asked by BBC television producer Phillip Lewis to devise an eight-week snooker programme. Colour had added a new dimension to television and one sport likely to benefit was snooker. Ted went away and came back with the idea of 'Pot Black'. Lewis liked it and Lowe went out and assembled the eight invited professionals . . . which wasn't too difficult a job because there weren't too many to pick from at the time!

That was the foundation on which the great sport of today was built and there is no doubting Ted Lowe's enormous contribution. His knowledge of the sport is second to none, and let's hope he keeps whispering behind that microphone for many years to come.

'Mr Snooker', commentator Ted Lowe. Ted played a large part in the birth of televised snooker in 1969 when he was responsible for arranging the first 'Pot Black' tournament

JACK McLAUGHLIN

Born: 29 January 1959, Belfast, Northern Ireland

Turned professional: 1984

First ranking points: 1986 Rothmans Grand Prix

Like Alex Higgins, Jack McLaughlin was born in Belfast. And like Higgins he made the journey across the Irish Sea to a Manchester base. It was while playing in the tough Manchester 'school' of snooker that McLaughlin established himself as a good class amateur. He won the Northern Ireland amateur title in successive years in 1983 and 1984 and in the second of those years came close to winning the English amateur title but lost to Steve Longworth in the northern area final. So disappointed was Jack at losing that he promptly announced he was quitting the game. It must be one of the shortest retirements on record . . . it lasted 45 minutes!

An established Northern Ireland amateur international, he turned professional in 1984 and had to wait until his third season

CAREER HIGHLIGHTS

1983-84
Northern Ireland Amateur Champion

1986
Rothmans Grand Prix (last 32)

1987
Dulux British Open (last 32)

1988
Irish Professional Champion

Rankings
Year	Ranking
1985	69
1986	71
1987	50
1988	64

before producing some of the form he had shown in his amateur days. Jack collected his first ranking point in the 1986 Rothmans but Jimmy White made sure he took only one point home, as the Londoner won 5-2, but McLaughlin was certainly not disgraced in defeat.

Beats his idol

Another ranking point came Jack's way later in the season and it helped him jump 20 places up the rankings. This time the point was for reaching the last 32 of the Dulux British Open and the man he beat to qualify for the third round was none other than his idol, Alex Higgins. Fellow Mancunian David Taylor thwarted Jack's progress to the next round.

In early 1988 Jack was the surprise winner of the Irish professional title, beating Dennis Taylor in the final.

In 1988 Jack McLaughlin ended the domination of Alex Higgins and Dennis Taylor by beating Taylor to win the Irish Professional title for the first time

MURDO McLEOD

Born: 14 January 1947, Edinburgh, Scotland

Turned professional: 1981

First ranking points: 1982 Professional Players Tournament

CAREER HIGHLIGHTS

1983-85
Scottish Professional Champion

1987
Embassy World Professional Championship (last 16)

1988
MIM Britannia British Open (last 16)

Rankings
Year	Ranking
1983	27
1984	29
1985	26
1986	22
1987	30
1988	48

Stephen Hendry may be the current 'golden boy' of Scottish snooker, but Murdo McLeod holds a unique place in Scottish snooker history. When he beat Rex Williams 10-7 in the first round of the Embassy in 1987 he became the first ever Scot to win a match at the Crucible. For Murdo, it was his second appearance at Sheffield, and his first win in ten television appearances.

The victory at Sheffield marked the end of a traumatic season for Murdo. His father, to whom he was very close, died at the start of the season. Murdo then moved house, and his wife Anne presented the McLeod household with bairn number four!

Murdo loses a friend

Although he is one of the most popular men on the professional circuit, his morale was at rock bottom. Losing his father devastated him, reflected by his poor results, but at the Crucible in Sheffield, it was if he was winning for his dad.

A former baker, Murdo was brought up in Edinburgh and was an all-round sportsman as a youngster. He was a good tennis player and played Scottish Junior League football, just a couple of steps down from League soccer, until a knee injury ended his career.

He started playing the more sedate game of snooker when he was 14. After playing Alex Higgins in an exhibition, which the Irishman won 4-3, Murdo reflected how close he had come to beating the former world champion, and decided he would apply for professional status.

A Scottish international since 1975, he was accepted as a professional in 1981. He twice won the Scottish Professional title by beating Eddie Sinclair in the final, but in the ranking tournaments could not get beyond the last 16, the stage he reached in the Goya, Coral UK Open and Dulux British Open in 1985-86, earning six valuable ranking points and lifting himself to 22nd in the rankings.

He was managed by Ian Doyle until they parted company in 1987, when Murdo teamed up with Rob Thallon, the owner of a chain of Edinburgh fashion stores. In a bad season in 1987–88 Murdo slipped down the rankings but he still has that moment of glory at the Crucible to savour . . . forever.

One of the game's nice guys, Scotland's Murdo Mcleod, so often on the verge of success

DAVE MARTIN

Born: 9 May 1948, Wheatley Hill, County Durham, England

Turned professional: 1981

First ranking points: 1983 Jameson International

Dave Martin emerged as the surprise semi-finalist in the 1981 Jameson International at Derby's Assembly Rooms. Wins over Bill Werbeniuk and Eddie Charlton put him in the last four against Dennis Taylor. Despite losing heavily the name of Dave Martin was established on the professional circuit.

Those who watched him as an amateur were not surprised at Dave's success in his first full season as a professional. An international in 1979 and 1980, he was the beaten finalist in the English Amateur Championship in both those years, losing to Jimmy White and Joe O'Boye respectively.

Success doesn't breed success

He was finally accepted as a professional by the WPBSA in January 1981. His first event was that year's World Championship, and the following season he made that terrific impact on his second professional tournament. Dave openly admits he made the mistake of sitting back and resting on that 'success' in the Jameson. He thought the winning would come automatically, and he expected the bookings to roll in because of the television exposure. He was wrong. He realised he had still to work hard at the game, and any young up-and-coming player should heed the warning of Dave's complacency.

Mike Watterson's Snookersport agency looked after Dave's affairs for a while, and Watterson installed him as the resident professional at the Sheffield Snooker Club. But the arrangement did not last long after he found himself involved in too many off-the-table activities. Dave was on his own again. He decided he would try and live off his tournament winnings and spend as much

CAREER HIGHLIGHTS
1978
National Pairs Champion (with D. Reed)
1981
Jameson International (semi-final)
1984
Yamaha International Masters (runner-up)

Rankings	
1983	29
1984	26
1985	29
1986	28
1987	27
1988	36

Although he has never been able to break into the top 16 Dave Martin has been a consistent player

time as he could practising at either the Master Club in Nottingham, or the Clay Cross Snooker Centre. Since 1978 Steve Davis's mentor Frank Callan has helped Dave with some coaching.

Hard work rewarded

In 1984, having worked very hard at his game, Dave was back at the Derby Assembly Rooms, this time in the Yamaha International, and he surprised a few more people by reaching the three-man round-robin final alongside Steve Davis and John Dunning, an even bigger surprise finalist than himself. After coming through a tough semi-final group containing Ray Reardon and Eddie Charlton, Martin opened the final by beating Dunning. The title eventually hinged on the outcome between Davis and Martin which the former won easily 3-0. But once again, the name of Dave Martin was up there alongside the top names of the game.

Despite not enjoying similar success since then, Dave had one of his best wins in the 1988 Mercantile Credit Classic when he beat Jimmy White 5-2 to reach the last 8. Those three ranking points kept him within striking range of the top 32.

TONY MEO

Born: 4 October 1959, Hampstead, London, England

Turned professional: 1979

First ranking points: 1981 Embassy World Professional Championship

What do Tony Meo and Jimmy White have in common? Quite a lot really. They are both exceptional snooker players, both are left-handers, both are members of the Barry Hearn stable, and both used to be in the same class at the Ernest Bevin Comprehensive school.

As a 13-year-old Meo had a difficult decision to make: either to go to Italy with his parents or stay in London with friends. He chose

> **'It's funny, when I had nothing I never used to worry about anything. But now I've got plenty of money I worry all the time.'**
>
> *A confession from Tony Meo*
>
> *After thieves broke into Tony's house and stole many mementos he said*
>
> **'Lucky they didn't steal anything important like my cue.'**

the latter. Meo and his schoolmate White spent a lot of time together outside school hours at Zans Billiard Hall. They were 'managed' by local taxi driver Bob Davis who used to ferry them around the country to play money matches. They got too good for Bob to handle, and they teamed up with Patsy Fagan under Henry West's wing.

In 1976 Tony became, at 17, the youngest person ever to compile a maximum break, a feat he performed while playing against current professional Terry Whitthread. Tony beat Jimmy to win the 1977 Junior Pontins title and the following year he beat twice-winner Ian Williamson to win the National Under-19 title. In 1979, after winning all his four matches

Tony Meo after retaining the English Professional Championship in 1987; it is the only major individual title Meo has won

CAREER HIGHLIGHTS

1978
National Under-19 Champion

1981
Winfield Australian Masters Champion

1982
Hofmeister World Doubles Champion (with Steve Davis)

1983
Hofmeister World Doubles Champion (with Steve Davis)
State Express World Team Classic (member of England team)

1984
Lada Classic (runner-up)

1985
Winfield Australian Masters Champion
Hofmeister World Doubles Champion (with Steve Davis)

1986
Tolly Cobbold English Professional Champion
Hofmeister World Doubles Champion (with Steve Davis)

1987
Tolly Cobbold English Professional Champion

Rankings

Year	Ranking
1983	15
1984	10
1985	10
1986	11
1987	20
1988	31

for England in the Home International Championship, Tony turned professional.

Brilliant potter

It was not long before Tony was attracting a lot of attention. His potting was superb and in his first year he reached the Crucible stage of the World Championship, losing only narrowly 10-9 to Alex Higgins. A season later he beat the defending champion, John Virgo,

9-1 in the Coral UK Championship, before losing to Steve Davis in the quarter-final. In the English Professional Championship he reached his first final, but again it was Davis who had the upper hand, winning 9-3.

Meo joined Davis in the Barry Hearn stable in 1982 and the two men teamed up for that year's Hofmeister World Doubles title. They won it, and have proved almost invincible at doubles play. But Davis continued to be Tony's scourge in individual events. In the 1984 Lada Classic at Warrington Tony had his best chance to date of lifting a major individual title and it was Davis who spoiled the party

---

'I am dazed. It has taken a long time to win a major title but it has all been worth waiting for.'

Meo after winning the 1986 English Professional Championship

---

by winning 9-8. Tony had victory in his grasp and had a simple yellow followed by the colours for victory when somebody in the crowd shouted 'Come on, Tony'. It spoilt his concentration and he missed the yellow. Davis won the frame and went on to win the match.

An individual title at last

Steve also won 9-8 in the semi-final of the 1985 Tolly Cobbold English Professional Championship at Ipswich but it was in that event, in 1986, that Tony gained his first major individual win in Britain, albeit in a non-ranking tournament. He had, however, won abroad when he won the Winfield Australian Masters in 1981 and 1985, but beating Neal Foulds in the final of the Tolly Cobbold English Professional was the highlight of Tony's career. He successfully defended the title a year later when he beat the surprise finalist Les Dodd.

It looks as though another Tony Meo pot is on its way

Tony has never fared too well in the World Championship, a quarter-final defeat by Tony Knowles in 1983 being his best result. In recent years Liverpool's John Parrott has been Meo's stumbling block. He beat Tony in the first round in 1986 and when Parrott knocked him out again at the first hurdle a year later it meant Tony was out of the top 16 in the rankings for the first time in five years, and was the only member of the Barry Hearn troupe not to figure in the top 16.

Tony has a reputation for being a 'natty' dresser. He is also one of the best natured players on the circuit. A firm believer in the family, Tony spends his relaxation hours with his wife and kids, or playing cricket when wife Denise lets him. A useful all-rounder, he is the Ian Botham of the snooker world.

GRAHAM MILES

Born: 11 May 1941, Birmingham, England

Turned professional: 1969

First ranking points: 1974 World Professional Championship

In the mid-1970s Graham Miles was, along with Ray Reardon, John Spencer and Eddie Charlton, one of the world's outstanding players. Very distinctive in his style, with his chin resting on the cue, he was not in awe of any of his opponents and was a tough player to beat.

Twice the Midlands Amateur Champion and the 1966 National Breaks Champion, Graham, a former diesel fitter with the Birmingham Corporation, decided to turn professional in 1969. In those days championships were few and far between and Graham relied on the exhibition and holiday camp circuits to earn his living. He reached the quarter-final of the 1973 World Professional Championship at the City Exhibition Hall, Manchester, but lost to the eventual finalist Eddie Charlton.

'Pot Black' invitation . . . Graham's big break

That success led Graham to be invited as a late replacement for the 1974 'Pot Black' series when Fred Davis withdrew. Graham went on to beat Eddie Charlton, John Spencer and Ray Reardon to win the final and the following year he successfully retained the title. That exposure helped develop his popularity on the exhibition circuit and Miles made a comfortable living from the sport.

He reached the final of the World Championship at Belle Vue in 1974 but was on the receiving end of a 22-12 win by Ray Reardon. But, wherever he played, Miles was regarded as a threat to the band of already established professionals. He played Reardon in the final of the 1976 Benson & Hedges Masters but, again, Rear-

don came out the winner. John Spencer beat Miles in the final of the Holsten Lager tournament in 1979 but in 1981, when Miles was on a downward trend, he temporarily halted the slide by winning the invitational Tolly Cobbold Classic, beating Cliff Thorburn 5-1. That was Graham's last win on the professional circuit and, as the number of professionals increases, he is finding it hard to qualify for ranking events.

Ranked fifth in the world in 1976, he was still among the top 16 in 1980 but since then has slid dramatically out of the top 32. He has not qualified for the final world championship stages since 1984.

Graham owns two snooker clubs, one at Sandwell, West Midlands and one at Crewe, Cheshire.

Graham Miles had a lucky break in being invited to compete on 'Pot Black' in 1974. You never know, another lucky break could just see him winning again.

CAREER HIGHLIGHTS

1974
World Professional Championship (runner-up)
'Pot Black' Champion

1975
'Pot Black' Champion

1981
Tolly Cobbold Classic Champion

Rankings
Year	Ranking
1983	22
1984	32
1985	32
1986	56
1987	68
1988	65

In the mid-1970s Birmingham's Graham Miles was one of the deadliest of potters. In 1974 he came very close to winning the world title but was thwarted in the final by Ray Reardon who won 22–12 at Manchester's Belle Vue

DOUG MOUNTJOY

Born: 8 June 1942, Tir-y-Berth, Glamorgan, Wales

Turned professional: 1976

First ranking points: 1977 Embassy World Professional Championship

Despite the influx of so much new young talent Welshman Doug Mountjoy has maintained his consistency and until 1988 remained a member of the 'top 16 club' in the world rankings. Even though he has not reached the final of a ranking tournament since the 1981 World Championship he has continued to be a tough player to beat and regularly has good results in the ranking events.

A former miner, Mountjoy was brought up just outside Ebbw Vale. He was a well known snooker player in the valleys, where so many great players developed over the years. He gained his first national notice in 1974 when he

---

After having to watch her 10-year-old son play Terry Griffiths' son in the first round of the 1982 Junior Pontins Championship Yvonne Mountjoy said

'This is worse than watching Doug play.'

---

travelled to Prestatyn – to win the coveted Pontins Open trophy. Receiving 25 points per frame from experienced professional John Spencer, Doug became the first amateur to win a £1,000 first prize in snooker.

Late entrant . . . surprise winner

Doug had won the Welsh amateur title in 1968 and after winning the title again in 1976 he was eligible to represent Wales at the World Amateur Championships in Johannesburg. He was in devastating form as he lifted the title with a record 11-1 win in the final over Malta's Paul Mifsud. On returning home he turned professional and received a late invitation to the Benson & Hedges Masters at the London Theatre, Drury Lane – his first professional tournament. To everyone's surprise, probably even Doug's, he beat Alex Higgins in the semi-final before beating fellow-Welshman Ray Reardon 7-6 in the final. A couple of months

later he beat Higgins again in the first round of the World Championship but lost 13-11 to Dennis Taylor in the quarter-final.

No player can boast such a great start to his professional career and Doug started off the next season where he left off by reaching the final of the inaugural Super Crystalate United Kingdom Championship at Blackpool. John Spencer fell in his wake in the second round and in the semi-final Higgins suffered his third defeat in their three meetings before losing to Patsy Fagan. In the same event, renamed the Coral UK Championship a year later, Doug went one better and won the title by beating David Taylor 15-9 in the final. He beat Reardon 6-5 to win the Benson & Hedges Irish Masters later in the season and beat Reardon again to win the first of his four Welsh professional titles at the start of 1980.

The success story of Doug Mountjoy seemed to be coming to an end in 1981. The season started with Doug suffering an illness that left part of his face paralysed, but fortunately the problem cleared up. He arrested a slide downhill with a great run in the Embassy, beating Eddie Charlton, Dennis Taylor and Reardon, yet again, to book a final meeting with Steve Davis, who went on to win his first title 18-12. Against Reardon Doug enjoyed one of his great moments in snooker when he compiled a 145 break to create a new championship record.

Doug Mountjoy . . . mine host

After that run Doug's only successes for a while were in beating Terry Griffiths to win the 1982 Welsh professional title and to beat Cliff Wilson to capture the same title in 1984. After acquiring the Temple Bar public house near Hereford, complete with snooker table, Doug got down to some

The 1977 World Amateur champion, Doug Mountjoy has since enjoyed a successful professional career and was world championship runner-up

practice and it had immediate effect with him reaching the quarter-final of the 1985 Rothmans Grand Prix and the final of the Benson & Hedges Masters, the tournament that gave him his first triumph eight years earlier. This time he came away empty handed, beaten by Cliff Thorburn.

Since then, apart from reaching three Welsh Professional finals (beating Steve Newbury to win his fourth title in 1987) Doug's best result was in reaching the semi-final of the 1986 Mercantile Credit Classic. He reached that stage in unusual circumstances when his quarter-final opponent Neal Foulds went in-off the respotted black to give the frame and match to Doug. In the semi there was no such good fortune for the Welshman as Cliff Thorburn beat him 9-6. But results like that have been sufficient to keep Doug among the top-ranked players. Late in 1986 however, Doug suffered the embarrassment of the biggest defeat of his career when Lancastrian Steve Longworth ousted him from the Tennents UK Open 9-1.

Doug Mountjoy is too good to be in the wilderness for long. If he does come back and show the match-winning tenacity he did in his early days as a professional, few people will begrudge him his success, because he has worked hard at his game.

Doug Mountjoy holding the Coral UK Professional Championship trophy after beating David Taylor 15-9 to win the title in 1978. It is the only the only major individual professional tournament the Welshman has won

CAREER HIGHLIGHTS

1968
Welsh Amateur Champion

1976
Welsh Amateur Champion
World Amateur Champion

1977
Benson & Hedges Masters
Champion

1978
Coral UK Champion
Benson & Hedges Irish
Masters Champion
State Express World Team
(member of winning Wales
team)

1980
Welsh Professional Champion
State Express World Team
(member of winning Wales
team)

1981
Embassy World Professional
Championship (runner-up)

1982
Welsh Professional Champion

1984
Welsh Professional Champion

1987
Welsh Professional Champion

Rankings

Year	Ranking
1983	12
1984	15
1985	15
1986	14
1987	14
1988	24

TOMMY MURPHY

Born: 8 January 1962, Newtownards, County Down, Northern Ireland

Turned professional: 1981

First ranking points: 1985 Goya International

CAREER HIGHLIGHTS

1980
National Under-19 Champion

1981
Northern Ireland Amateur Champion

1987
Dulux British Open (last 16)

1988
Mercantile Credit Classic (last 16)

Rankings

1983	–	1986	57
1984	55	1987	44
1985	56	1988	42

If sheer hard work were good enough to lift a player up the rankings then Irishman Tommy Murphy would figure high up that list. Hardworking, and very capable, Tommy has not had the breaks he has deserved in his years as a professional.

Born in Newtownards, Tommy first started playing snooker at the St Patrick's Social Club when he was 14. His first mentor was Brian Orr, and Tommy soon developed into a top-class youngster. At 18 he won the British Under-19 title, following in the footsteps of Joe Johnson, Tony Knowles, and Tony Meo. A year later, in 1981, Tommy won the Northern Ireland Amateur title and that same year turned professional. In the August he made the decision to move to England and initially settled in Sheffield before moving to Loughborough.

His first job was at the Loughborough Snooker Centre but he is now based at Chalkies in Thurmaston, near Leicester. But Tommy still lives at Loughborough with wife Linda and their two children, Darren and Kelly. Linda acts as Tommy's manager, accountant, road manager etc.

The ex-apprentice coffin maker enjoyed the best win of his professional career in the 1988 Mercantile Credit Classic when he beat Dean Reynolds 5-4 in the fourth round.

Great boost in 1987

A middle-ranked player, Tommy made a jump of 13 places in 1986-87 thanks to two well-earned points from the Dulux British Open, where he reached the last 16 before losing to Tony Knowles. But a 5-4 defeat of Ray Reardon in the previous round was a creditable performance.

Tommy received a big boost in 1987 when he was selected to represent the Northern Ireland team in the 1988 World Team Championship, replacing Eugene Hughes as partner to Alex Higgins and Dennis Taylor. That alone has helped boost Tommy's confidence and he has set his sights on getting into the top 32 – 'If not this year, then maybe next', he says. If he continues working hard there should be no problem about him reaching his goal.

Irish-born Tommy Murphy is now based in Loughborough

STEVE NEWBURY

Born: 21 April 1956, Neath, Glamorgan, Wales

Turned professional: 1984

First ranking points: 1984 Jameson International

Despite many great moments in his long and successful career as an amateur, and now as a professional, the one moment from snooker that gave him the biggest thrill was in representing Wales at the 1980 World Amateur Championships at Australia. He lost in the quarter-final to the eventual winner Jimmy White, but the honour of representing his country at the championships will last forever.

A very talented amateur and Welsh International, he played in eight successive Home International Championships and in 1980 won the Welsh national title. He had reached the final two years earlier but lost to Alwyn Lloyd. On the way to the 1978 final Steve beat Terry Griffiths which persuaded Terry to turn professional because there was no chance of him playing in the World Amateur Championship. Steve did Terry a favour . . . 12 months later Griffiths was the World Professional Champion.

Totally dedicated

Steve started his snooker at Mackworth's in Neath, the starting point for many of Wales' top players. Mario Berni and Viv Rosser were early influences on his career. His decision to turn professional in 1984 came at a time when he was invincible in the amateur game, but he made the right decision and in his first professional event he collected £3,000 for reaching the last 32 of the Jameson International.

He reached the final of the 1987 Welsh Professional Championship before losing 9-7 to Doug Mountjoy. Then he started the 1987-88 season by reaching the last 32 of the Fidelity before Cliff Thorburn ended any further celebrations. But in the next ranking tournament, the Rothmans Grand Prix at Reading, Steve had his best result in a ranking tournament when he reached the last eight. Dennis Taylor eventually put Steve out, but Steve had the satisfaction of a revenge 5-0 whitewash of Thorburn two rounds earlier.

Another win over Thorburn, followed by successes over Martin Clark and Terry Griffiths put Steve in his first major semi-final in the 1988 Mercantile. He lost 9-2 to Steve Davis but edged his way close to a top-16 position in the rankings. He disappointingly lost 10-8 to Barry West in the 1988 World Championship qualifying rounds.

CAREER HIGHLIGHTS

1979
National Pairs Champion
(with Cliff Wilson)

1980
Welsh Amateur Champion

1987
Welsh Professional
Championship (runner-up)

1988
Mercantile Credit Classic
(semi-final)

Rankings
Year	Ranking
1985	34
1986	40
1987	45
1988	25

Newbury showed his full talent in reaching the Welsh Professional Championship final in 1987

JOE O'BOYE

Born: 6 March 1960, Leicester, England

Turned professional: 1985

First ranking points: 1985 Rothmans Grand Prix

CAREER HIGHLIGHTS

1979
National Under-19 Champion

1980
English Amateur Champion

1987
Irish Professional
Championship (runner-up)
Fidelity Unit Trusts
International (quarter-final)

1988
MIM Britannia British Open
(quarter-final)

Rankings
1986	65
1987	55
1988	35

Joe O'Boye was the under-19 Champion in 1979 and the following year succeeded Jimmy White as English Amateur Champion. In those days, such creditable performances would have been good enough to warrant a successful application to join the professional ranks. But O'Boye was refused – three times. Despite his excellent playing record there was another side to O'Boye. He gained the reputation for being the 'Wild Man of Snooker', particularly after heavy drinking bouts, and his reputation led to the WPBSA declining his applications, despite his obvious playing ability.

He is the oldest of three brothers, one of whom, Vince, was a professional boxer. Joe's first love was snooker and he started playing at Osbornes in Leicester, Willie Thorne's early grooming ground. A very talented player, speedy round the table, O'Boye is cool when under pressure.

Gordon Banks – snooker manager

Many men tried to put O'Boye on the 'straight and narrow' and failed. One was the former England goalkeeper Gordon Banks who managed Joe in 1982. But even he could not sort him out. Eventually O'Boye saw the error of his ways and sorted himself out. He moved to the Kings Cross Snooker Centre in 1984 and the following year was eventually accepted as a professional.

On his television debut Joe impressed, despite losing 5-4 to Jimmy White after leading 4-2 in the last 32 of the Rothmans Grand Prix.

Joe seems to like the Rothmans

'I don't regret anything – you're only young once and you can't buy youth.'

Joe about his reckless days as a youngster

---

event because he picked up another ranking point the following season when, again, he reached the last 32. This time he lost to Welshman Steve Newbury, but he had claimed the notable scalp of Cliff Thorburn in the pre-televised stage.

O'Boye ended his second professional season by moving up the rankings ten places and by reaching the final of the Irish Professional Championship, for which he is eligible because of his parentage. Defending champion Dennis Taylor was too good for Joe on the day. But he has proved in his first two years as a professional that his 'Wild Man' image has gone and the great talent from his amateur days is going to stand him in good stead for the future.

He started the 1987–88 season by reaching the last eight of the Fidelity at Stoke on Trent. In the 1988 Irish Professional Championship he beat Alex Higgins in the quarter-final.

The one-time 'wild man' of snooker, Joe O'Boye has quietened down in recent years and the transformation is paying dividends on the snooker table

DENE O'KANE

Born: 24 February 1963, Christchurch, New Zealand

Turned professional: 1984

First ranking points: 1985 Dulux British Open

When New Zealander Dene O'Kane reached the quarter-final of the Embassy World Championship in 1987 it was a well-deserved and welcome return from the wilderness.

He was the New Zealand Amateur Snooker Champion at 17. The British fans got their first glimpse of O'Kane the following year when he was invited to appear in the inaugural 'Junior Pot Black' and he finished runner-up to Dean Reynolds. Having spent a lot of time in Britain developing his game, he represented New Zealand in the 1982 World Amateur Championship at Calgary, Canada. He started as one of the favourites but failed to qualify for the final stages.

O'Kane turned professional in 1984 and at the end of his first season had made the top 32 in the rankings by reaching the first round proper of the Jameson and the quarter-final of the Dulux British Open, losing 5-1 to Steve Davis.

Early snooker with a broom handle and ping-pong balls

He reached the Crucible stage of the World Championship at the first attempt, to become the first New Zealander to play at the famous venue. Sadly Dene lost 10-4 to David Taylor. It was a tremendous professional beginning for the youngster who started playing snooker at the age of 12 by using a broom handle and ping-pong balls on a table-tennis table. At 13 he was a regular player at the Takapuna Billiard Hall in Auckland, and, being under age, he was thrown out by the police more times than he can remember. But he still kept up with his education and left school with all his O-level equivalents. Dene's inspiration

came from watching Alex Higgins and John Spencer when they toured New Zealand in the 1970s, and the man responsible for arranging that tour, Fred Hawken, become Dene's first coach/manager.

If 1984-85 was a roaring success for Dene then his second season was a disaster. He won only one match in six ranking tournaments and had lost confidence in his own ability. He parted company with manager Peter Herod and teamed up with Cliff Thorburn in the Robert Winsor stable. 'One of the best things that ever happened to me', is how O'Kane described the move. It had the desired effect and he regained faith in his own ability. He started winning again, and the greatest moment of his professional career came when he reached the last eight of the World Championship at Sheffield.

Five centuries in the 1987 Embassy . . . and all before the Crucible

In the qualifying competition he played some of his best snooker and before he got to the Crucible he had compiled five century breaks including a 132 against Dave Gilbert and a 130 against Ian Black which were the two highest of the 1987 championship. In the first round he was paired with stablemate Thorburn, who raced into a 5-1 lead which O'Kane pulled back to 5-4 at the half-way stage. Dene continued the streak and made it nine successive frames to win 10-5. He then beat former finalist Doug Mountjoy 13-5 to earn a quarter-final place with Jimmy White. Having enjoyed two great wins he couldn't cope with the pressure of playing Jimmy and soon trailed 8-0. He courageously pulled that back to 11-5 but even-

Dene O'Kane showed remarkable composure when he beat Cliff Thorburn in the 1987 World Championship

tually went down 13-6. The £12,000 loser's cheque was ample compensation.

Dene spends hours practising, either at the new luxury Winners' Club in London, the Kentish Town Snooker Club or on the BCE table at Robert Winsor's home. O'Kane has the talent to win a major tournament, and he now has the security of Winsor's experience behind him.

CAREER HIGHLIGHTS

1980
New Zealand Amateur Champion

1987
Embassy World Professional Championship (quarter-final)

1988
MIM Britannia British Open (quarter-final)

Rankings
1985	32
1986	39
1987	35
1988	24

KEN OWERS

Born: 30 March 1953, Fleetwood, Lancashire, England

Turned professional: 1986

First ranking points: 1986 BCE International

Ken Owers may live in the fishing town of Fleetwood on the Fylde coast but contrary to popular belief he has never worked on the trawlers. In fact he served his apprenticeship with ICI as a fitter/turner.

He started playing snooker when he was 11 at the local Fleetwood Billiard Hall before moving on to the Fleetwood West End club which was Ken's snooker schooling ground. While at the West End he won the coveted Working Men's Club and Institute Union snooker title in 1986 by beating

Fleetwood is proud of its only professional, Ken Owers

Geoff Thomas. A year earlier Ken applied to be accepted as a professional but was rejected. However, he finished third in the new pro-ticket series that year and automatically became eligible to take

CAREER HIGHLIGHTS

1986
WMC & IU Champion
BCE International (last 16)

Ranking
1987   52
1988   53

up professional status at the start of the 1986-87 season . . . and what a great start he had to his new career.

Two Matchroom boys feel the full force of Ken's skill

Ken beat Jimmy White 5-2 in the second round of his first professional event, the BCE International. He followed that with a 5-0 whitewash of the talented New Zealander Dene O'Kane before Neal Foulds brought him back down to earth on his television debut. A revenge win over Foulds in the English Professional Championship later in the season was further proof that Ken Owers was not to be taken lightly by any of the professionals.

A fine attacking player, he has worked hard at developing his safety play since turning professional and he is a good all-round player. To pick up two ranking points in a first professional event is no mean feat in today's high calibre fields. Even before he turned professional, the attacking style of Ken Owers was in demand for exhibition matches, and Blackburn-based brewers Thwaites contracted him to do a series of exhibitions for them. He still does work for Thwaites and also provides exhibition matches in Belgium, which are organised by his manager, Ken Lowe of the Commonwealth Sporting Club in Blackpool, where Ken is the resident professional.

Married to Lynne, Ken has two children, Anthony and Suzanne.

'I didn't know I could play as well as that.'

Ken's comments after beating Jimmy White in the 1986 BCE International at Stoke-on-Trent

In Fleetwood they had a saying in 1987

'Ken Owers 2, Barry Hearn's lot 1 . . .'

Making reference to his wins over White and Foulds, and the one defeat by Foulds

JOHN PARROTT

Born: 11 May 1964, Liverpool, England

Turned professional: 1983

First ranking points: 1984 Lada Classic

At 24 in 1988 John Parrott was almost considered an 'old timer' in the world of professional snooker, because of the number of younger players, like Stephen Hendry and Martin Clark, in the professional ranks. Parrott's arrival on the professional scene in 1983-84 was as impressive as anybody's. In his third tournament, the Lada Classic at Warrington, he firmly told the snooker world that he had arrived.

Parrott v Higgins or Liverpool v Manchester United

Played not far from his Liverpool home, John had dozens of his own followers in the Spectrum Arena for that event, and when he was drawn against Alex Higgins the rivalry between the two sets of followers was reminiscent of a soccer match between Merseyside and Manchester. John completely outplayed Higgins and won 5-2.

He showed the same confidence and lack of fear of his next opponent, Tony Knowles, but then lost 5-4 to Steve Davis in a great semi-final, which John could well have won.

Tony Knowles fell victim to Parrott at the Crucible three months later before Dennis Taylor ended the youngster's dream with a 13-11 win in the second round. But John Parrott was a much talked about newcomer and he ended his first season at number 20 in the rankings.

John was born at Liverpool's Oxford Street maternity hospital. His parents split up when he was young and he lived with his father just off Penny Lane, the Liverpool street immortalised by the Beatles.

When he was 12 John was an

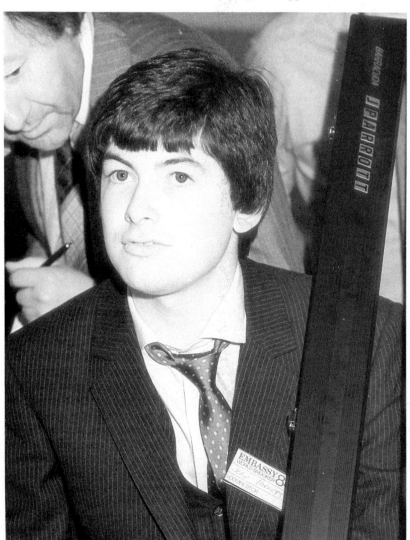

CAREER HIGHLIGHTS

1981
Pontins Junior Champion

1982
Pontins Open Champion
Junior 'Pot Black' Champion

1983
Junior 'Pot Black' Champion

1984
Lada Classic (semi-final)

1986
Tennents UK Open (semi-final)

1987
Rothmans Grand Prix (semi-final)

1988
Mercantile Credit Classic (runner-up)

Rankings
1984	20
1985	18
1986	17
1987	13
1988	7

John Parrott enjoyed his best-ever season in 1987–8 but despite coming so close, he could not register that first all-important win.

A great stylist, John Parrott has a solid all-round game

After beating Ray Reardon to win the 1982 Pontins Open in front of a 2,000 crowd John said

'I think this is where I belong'

John's dad nearly changed John's surname when he was a youngster from Parrott to Parr because of all the ribbing he got at school. It's a good job he didn't . . . Fleet Street would have been 'stuffed' otherwise! How could they have penned such headlines as

'SICK AS A PARR'

excellent bowls player but on holiday at nearby Southport fate played its role in creating John Parrott, snooker player.

From bowls to snooker . . . just because it rained

One day the weather was lousy and John's father Alan, a good league snooker player and capable of 40-50 breaks, took John into Nabs' Snooker Hall for a game. That was it . . . bowls went by the board and snooker took over and for two hours after school every day John used to practise. At 14 he played in the competitive Garston and District league. He made his first century (129 actually) when he was 16 and fate took another turn in John's favour. In the club that day was local businessman Phil Miller

and his son Duncan. They watched the break and Miller offered to look after John in a managerial capacity. That friendship and relationship still stands today. Miller and current professional George Scott, who acted as John's first coach, helped to produce a snooker star of the future.

John left school with six O-levels but discontinued his A-level studies after a year because the pull of snooker was too great.

One of the game's top amateurs

As an amateur John had a good record which could have been even more impressive had he not fallen at the final hurdle several times. He lost to Terry Whitthread in the final of the Under-16 Championship in 1980 and two years later lost to Neal Foulds in the Under-19 final. But that year he beat Ray

Reardon to win the Pontins Open, after being the Pontins Junior Champion the year before.

In 1983 John was regarded as one of the best amateurs in the country and when he reached the final of the English Amateur Championship he was favourite to beat Tony Jones, but again he could not clear that final obstacle as Jones ran out the 13-9 winner. Nevertheless, John took up his professional status later that year, and as we have seen, fully justified such a move as he became a respected and feared member of the professional game. Since that glorious first season John has steadily risen up the rankings and now holds his place in the top eight.

The highlight of his second season was to reach the quarter-final of the Embassy World Professional Championship where he fought a great battle with the former champion Ray Reardon before the Welshman won 13-12.

A quarter-final appearance in the following season's Goya and reaching the second round of the Embassy were enough to take John up the rankings in 1986 to number 17, an agonising one place away from the advantageous top 16. But in 1986-87 he reached his goal, thanks to a great run in the Tennents UK Open when he beat Joe Johnson 9-1, Steve Longworth 9-6 and Tony Knowles . . . yet again, to reach the semi-final when he came up against his old rival Neal Foulds. The Londoner was too

*After four seasons as a professional John Parrott climbed into the all-
important top 16. But then, after only one season, he made the jump even
further and into the top eight*

As Liverpool's leading player John Parrott has maintained the Merseyside tradition for producing top class sportsmen and women

good for Parrott on the day and ran out the 9-3 winner. John had totally changed his cue action in 1986 thanks to receiving help from Frank Callan, the man who acted as Steve Davis' mentor.

Top 16 at last

Higgins was Parrott's victim for the second time in his career in the Mercantile as John booked a quarter-final meeting with Steve Davis once more. Davis was again the winner, and again it was 5-4.

Parrott assured himself of that top 16 place by beating Tony Meo at the Crucible, a defeat which pushed Meo from 11th to 20th in the rankings. Meo's team-mate Jimmy White put the record straight by beating John 13-11 in the next round.

The 1987-88 season started off in similar style. Parrott reached the semi-final of the Rothmans Grand Prix at Reading where he met the new young pretender, Stephen Hendry who made a similar impact on the game to that of Parrott four years earlier. John had victory in sight but Hendry came back to win 9-7. Impressive wins over David Taylor, John Virgo, Dennis Taylor and Tony Knowles put John in his first major final in 1988 when he met Steve Davis in the final of the Mercantile. But, once more, when victory was there for the taking, Parrott let Davis win 13-11 after leading 11-10.

John went with the Framework team to China in 1988 and beat Jin Weheng, Tony Drago, Dean Reynolds and Martin Clark to win the Kent Cup.

When he is not playing snooker John is regularly seen on the golf course and is one of the best players among the professionals with a handicap of six, which is fast falling further. Every other Saturday afternoon, however, is reserved because John can be seen sitting in the stands watching his favourite football team, Liverpool.

His great first season

John Parrott's first professional season was in 1983-84 and he claimed some notable scalps:

	Round	Opponent (Ranking)	Score
Professional Players Tournament	First	Patsy Fagan (25)	5-2
Lada Classic	Qualifying	Doug Mountjoy (12)	5-4
Lada Classsic	First	Alex Higgins (5)	5-2
Lada Classic	Second	Tony Knowles (4)	5-1
Embassy World Championship	Qualifying	Perrie Mans (17)	10-0
Embassy World Championship	First	Tony Knowles (4)	10-7

JACKIE REA

Born: 6 April 1921, Dungannon, County Tyrone, Northern Ireland

Turned Professional 1947

First ranking points: None

After Fred Davis, Jackie Rea is snooker's longest serving professional. Despite being ranked below the 100-mark he is still very much part of the snooker scene, and his inclusion in a book like this is unquestioned because of his vast contribution to the game for 40 years.

The master of the exhibition match, Jackie Rea was a great entertainer, providing wit and humour of the kind now dispensed by such as John Virgo and Dennis Taylor. His array of jokes and trick shots were seen long before the average man-in-the-street knew what a plant, set, spider or rest was. Rea was lightning fast around the table and made Alex Higgins and Jimmy White look slow. People love watching him play.

Jackie was Ireland's leading player and he held the Irish Professional title for 20 years until Alex Higgins came along and dethroned him in 1972. Alex and Jack both made the journey across the Irish Sea to bases around Manchester, and Jack still lives at Cheadle, just outside the city.

Beat Joe Davis to win the News of the World title

Rea started playing snooker in his father's pub at Dungannon when he was nine. He progressed to become the top amateur in Northern Ireland and after winning the Amateur title in 1947 immediately turned professional. Less than a year later he was the Northern Ireland Professional Champion as well.

In the declining days of snooker in the 1950s Jack won the coveted *News of the World* title in 1955, beating Joe Davis into second place. Two years later he was runner-up to John Pulman in the Professional Match-Play Championship, the world championship of the day in all but name. When 'Pot Black' started, Rea was an obvious choice for inclusion, and those television appearances only enhanced his exhibition demands.

There is nobody who would deny Jack any success that came his way in the new tough world of the professional game. But if any comes or not, there is one record that can never be taken

away from him. He holds the record for scoring the highest official break at Snooker-plus, 156. For his services to Snooker the WPBSA presented him with a special award at their presentation evening in 1987.

CAREER HIGHLIGHTS

1947
Northern Ireland Amateur Champion

1955
News of the World *Champion*

1947-50
Northern Ireland Professional Champion

1951-72
Northern Ireland Professional Champion

1957
World Professional Match-Play Championship (runner-up)

Rankings
Year	Ranking
1983	48
1984	61
1985	76
1986	103
1987	111
1988	99

'The short game's as good as ever, but anything over six feet and I'm struggling . . .'

Jack's self-confessed weakness, 1980

Jackie Rea holder of the Irish Professional title before Alex Higgins

RAY REARDON, MBE

Born: 8 October 1932, Tredegar, Monmouthshire, Wales

Turned Professional: 1968

First ranking points: 1974 World Professional Championship

Throughout the 1970s Ray Reardon was the biggest name in snooker and from the time world rankings were instituted in 1976 he was the undoubted number one until temporarily knocked off his perch by Cliff Thorburn in 1981. Reardon regained his top spot the following year but since then the influx of so many good new players, Ray's problems with his eyes, and domestic problems have led to his decline.

Born in Tredegar, Reardon followed local tradition by going down the mines when he was 14. In 1949 when he was 17 he won the *News of the World* amateur title and was presented with an ash cue by the late Joe Davis. With that cue Ray went on to win six world titles.

Buried alive for three hours

He was the toast of the valleys when he won the Welsh amateur title six years in succession in the early 1950s but he moved to Stoke-on-Trent when the Welsh pits started closing and he continued to work underground at the Florence Colliery. He was once involved in an accident and was buried alive for three hours. He didn't panic, and spent the time practising snooker shots in his mind. After that accident Reardon left the pits and joined the Stoke-on-Trent constabulary as PC184, and he won a commendation for disarming a man carrying a shotgun.

In 1964 Ray beat the man who was to become his great rival over the years, John Spencer, in the final of the English Amateur Championship. The following year he won the Working Men's Club and Institute Union title for the Cheadle Social Club. Offers of sponsorship came and in 1968 Reardon decided to turn professional. After winning his first world title at London's Victoria Hall in 1970 Ray was in big demand for exhibitions and on the holiday camp circuit. His winning of the inaugural 'Pot Black' competition the previous year had made him instantly recognisable, and Reardon and John Spencer were the first two men to capitalise on the snooker boom in the early 1970s.

A domination not seen for years

Reardon became popular because he added a touch of humour and entertainment to his game. But allied to that, his playing skill made him virtually unbeatable in the first half of the 1970s and his

In his hey-day Ray Reardon monopolised snooker as Steve Davis does today

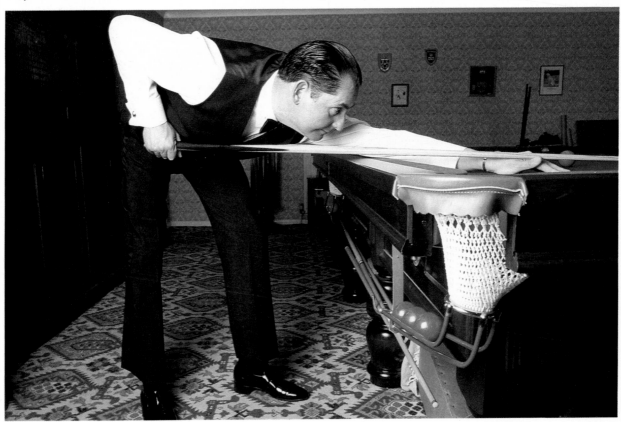

judgement of what shot to play made him a world beater. He was also a deadly long potter in his prime, and between 1972 and 1977 he played 17 world championship matches without defeat and won the title four years in succession.

He won his second title in 1973 at Manchester's City Exhibition Hall when he beat Eddie Charlton 38-32, but the match of the championship was the semi-final between Reardon and Spencer, which the Welshman won 23-22.

Reardon was not troubled in retaining the title the following year when he comfortably beat the up-and-coming Graham Miles 22-12 in the final at Belle Vue, Manchester. But when the championship was held in Melbourne in 1975 Reardon had a tough quarter-final with Spencer, which he won 19-17. He then beat Alex Higgins 19-14 before meeting the local hero Eddie Charlton in the final. Rear-

Ray's nickname is 'Dracula' . . . it was given to him by television's Paul Daniels after Ray appeared on one of his shows

Ray holds a unique double in broadcasting history. In 1976 he was the first snooker player to appear on 'This is Your Life' and in 1979 was the first to appear on 'Desert Island Discs'

Ray was honoured with the MBE in 1985. When he went to the Palace to collect his honour the Queen asked

'. . . and what do you do?'

. . . obviously Her Majesty is not a snooker fan!

CAREER HIGHLIGHTS

1950-55
Welsh Amateur Champion

1964
English Amateur Champion

1965
WMC & IU Champion

1970
World Professional Champion

1973-76
World Professional Champion

1976
Benson & Hedges Masters Champion

1978
World Professional Champion

1979-80
State Express World Team Classic (member of winning Wales team)

1981
Welsh Professional Champion

1982
Professional Players Tournament Champion

1983
Yamaha International Masters Champion
Welsh Professional Champion

Rankings

Year	Ranking
1983	2
1984	5
1985	6
1986	15
1987	38
1988	40

Ray Reardon, six times world champion in the 1970s, last won a major tournament in 1983

His great World Championship record

Between 1970 and 1978 Ray Reardon won the world title six times. His worst performance in that period was in reaching the quarter-final. This is his great record during that period:

1970 (Apr)	Final	John Pulman	won	39-34
1970 (Nov)	Semi-final	John Spencer	lost	15-34
1972	Quarter-final	Rex Williams	lost	23-25
1973	Final	Eddie Charlton	won	38-32
1974	Final	Graham Miles	won	22-12
1975	Final	Eddie Charlton	won	31-30
1976	Final	Alex Higgins	won	27-16
1977	Quarter-final	John Spencer	lost	6-13
1978	Final	Perrie Mans	won	25-18

In that period Reardon played a total of 30 matches in the championship, winning 27 and losing 3.
Only two men have beaten Reardon twice in the World Championship: Spencer, as above, and Steve Davis in 1985 and 1987.

score was 15-all. Higgins pulled away to win 18-15.

Since his last World Championship win Ray has twice won the Welsh Professional title, beating Cliff Wilson in the 1981 final and Doug Mountjoy in 1983. The only ranking event Reardon has won, other than the World Championship, was the 1982 Professional Players Tournament, when he beat one of the game's up-and-coming starlets, Jimmy White, 10-5 in the final at Birmingham's La Reserve club.

Reardon represented Wales in all the World Team Championships from their inauguration in 1979 to 1987 and was part of the winning combination that first

don ran out the 31-30 winner in a great battle that could have gone either way. It looked as though Charlton would win when 29-23 ahead but Reardon won seven frames on the trot to lead 30-29. Charlton levelled it at 30-all before Reardon won the final frame.

Ray won his fifth world title at Wythenshawe, Manchester in 1976 when he won the first Embassy-sponsored event. The organisation of the championship was a disaster but Reardon had little difficulty in beating Alex Higgins 27-16 in the final, after comfortably beating John Dunning, Dennis Taylor and Perrie Mans in the earlier rounds.

World title number six

In the next year's competition John Spencer became the first man since Rex Williams in 1972 to beat Reardon in the championship but in 1978 the Welshman came back to win his sixth world title. This time it was in the surroundings of Sheffield's Crucible Theatre, staging its second World Championship, and Reardon came through his early rounds without too much trouble before beating the South African Perrie Mans 25-18 in the final.

Reardon has appeared in only one final since then, in 1982 when he pushed Alex Higgins all the way until making a mistake when the

year and again in 1980. The highlight of Ray's career in recent years was to reach the final of the Hofmeister World Doubles Championship in 1985 with England's Tony Jones. After a great semi-final win over Terry Griffiths and Dennis Taylor, another Matchroom duo, Davis and Meo, put paid to the ambitions of the two outsiders by winning the final 12-5.

Ray's last individual title was in the 1983 Yamaha Organs International Masters when he beat Steve Davis in his qualifying group to get through to a second final meeting with Jimmy White. Reardon came from 6-4 down to win 9-6 and take the £12,000 first prize.

ORLD SNOOKER

Above: Reardon and Alex Higgins prepare to do battle in the 1982 World Championship final. After a great match the Irishman beat Ray 18-15

Left: Reardon seen with John Spencer, his great rival of the 1960s and 1970s. Between them they won every world title, except one, between 1969 and 1978

Things started going wrong for Ray in 1982 when his father died. He also developed poor sight and started wearing 'Dennis Taylor-style' spectacles, switching to contact lenses in 1987. In 1985 there were strong rumours about the break up of his 27-year marriage to Sue. He was eventually divorced and subsequent press coverage about his domestic problems could not have helped his play. But he is now settled and has moved south to set up home with his new wife, Carol.

Since 1983 Ray has dropped out of the top 32, but in the 1988 MIM Britannia British Open he beat Steve Davis 5-0, the first such defeat in Davis's professional career. Reardon hoped the corner had been turned, but he lost in the next round. He is still just in the top 40.

DEAN REYNOLDS

Born: 11 January 1963, Grimsby, Lincolnshire, England

Turned professional: 1981

First ranking points: 1982 Embassy World Professional Championship

When Dean Reynolds turned professional in 1981 he did not have a notable amateur career behind him, and was not even an England international, but he had already become a household name.

Having achieved notice in defeating New Zealander Dene O'Kane in the final of the inaugural 'Junior Pot Black' series he went on to beat the defending champion Tommy Murphy in the National Under-19 Championship before turning professional.

A gifted left-hander, Dean was accepted into the professional ranks and in his first professional tournament, the Embassy World Championship, he qualified for the Crucible after beating fellow Humbersider Ray Edmonds in the final qualifying stage. At Sheffield he played Fred Davis, the tournament's oldest player meeting the youngest . . . who won 10-7.

One of the many talented Humbersiders, Dean Reynolds

Silvino Francisco beat Reynolds in the next round but the youngster had shown the WPBSA were justified in accepting him into their ranks.

Encouraged by 'Butch' Reynolds

Dean first started showing an interest in snooker at the age of five when he used to accompany his dad 'Butch' to his local club. Dad is a good standard league player in the Grimsby area, but it was not long before the young Dean was showing signs of being able to beat him. At 12 he was beating some of the league's top players and in 1979 he won the Grimsby Boys' Championship and the Lincolnshire and South Humberside Junior Championship. By 17 he had earned a reputation for being a great break-builder and had more than 50 century breaks to his credit. But winning 'Junior Pot Black' sparked off his career.

In his first full season as a professional he claimed a notable scalp(!) in Willie Thorne in the 1982 Jameson International but the youngster was brought well down to earth in the next round when whitewashed 5-0 by Steve Davis. He reached the quarter-final of the Professional Players

CAREER HIGHLIGHTS

1981
Junior 'Pot Black' Champion
National Under-19 Champion

1987
Mercantile Credit Classic
(semi-final)

1988
English Professional
Champion

Rankings

Year	Ranking
1983	19
1984	22
1985	24
1986	29
1987	15
1988	22

Tournament before putting up a great fight in losing 9-8 to Alex Higgins in the Coral UK Championship. He ended his first full season by reaching the Crucible again, and once more he beat Ray Edmonds to earn the right to go to Sheffield, and it was Higgins who stopped the Humbersider's progress once more.

Another Davis 'whitewash'

The 1983-84 season brought home to Dean the stark realities of the professional game as he spent the season struggling. But he got back on the right track the following season when he beat the two Franciscos to reach the quarter-final of the Rothmans Grand Prix. However, Steve Davis then inflicted yet another 5-0 defeat on Dean.

Points in four of the six ranking events in 1985-86 helped consolidate Dean's position in the 17-32 group, but great runs in the BCE International, Tennent's UK Open and Mercantile Credit Classic saw him jump to number 15 the following season. Doug Mountjoy and David Taylor were swept aside by Reynolds in the BCE before Neal Foulds ended his run. In the Tennents, Silvino Francisco lost again to Dean before that man Davis did the damage in the next round. But happily it was not a whitewash this time as Davis won 9-5. But Dean's greatest performance since turning professional was in reaching the semi-final of the Mercantile.

Jimmy White flukes a red and wins

Excellent wins over Warren King and Cliff Thorburn were followed by successes over Barry West and

When losing the initiative after building up an 8-6 lead over Jimmy White in the 1987 World Championship Dean confessed

'I thought I'd done the hard work but I left Jimmy a few chances, and he took them.'

White won 10-8

Cliff Wilson. In the semi-final Dean had the daunting task of facing Jimmy White. In their only other professional meeting White had won 5-1. He won again this time but not until Dean had done himself proud in taking the Londoner the full 17 frames, to lose only when White fluked a red in the last frame to secure a 74 break and win the match. Reynolds gained compensation in the very next competition, the Professional

Reynolds, at last, won a major professional title in 1988 when he beat Neal Foulds to win the English Professional championship

Players Tournament, when he beat White 6-5. Unfortunately for Dean no ranking points were at stake.

White regained the upper hand in the World Championship a couple of months later when he won another great contest, this time 10-8, but he had to come back from being 8-6 down.

Dean teamed up with Alex Higgins, John Parrott and company in the Howard Kruger Framework empire in the summer of 1987. Early in 1988 he collected the biggest cheque of his career, £15,000, when he beat Neal Foulds in the final of the English Professional championship.

DAVID ROE

Born: 11 September 1965, Derby, England

Turned professional: 1986

First ranking point: Fidelity Unit Trusts International

CAREER HIGHLIGHTS

1987
Tennents UK Championship
(last 16)

1987
Fosters World Doubles (semi-final, with Steve James)

1988
MIM Britannia British Open
(last 16)

Ranking
1987   83
1988   39

David joined the professional ranks in 1986 as a result of finishing second to Jon Wright in the new Professional Ticket Tournaments the previous year. Roe won the first tournament, at Brean Sands, and finished runner-up to Wright in the second, at Pwllheli.

He made his first appearance in front of the cameras in 1987 after beating Doug Mountjoy in the last pre-televised stage of the Fidelity Unit Trusts International at Trentham Gardens, but he was beaten by Steve James.

Terry Whitthread, Mark Wildman and world number 27 Dave Martin all fell to Roe in the pre-televised stage of the Rothmans Grand Prix before Tony Knowles

David Roe; destined for the top?

prevented a first televised win.

Having disposed of 12th ranked Rex Williams, Roe beat Vic Harris 9–5 to reach the last 16 of a ranking tournament for the first time, but he was beaten in the next round by

Jimmy White 9-2.

Shortly afterwards David and Steve James reached the semi-final of the Fosters World Doubles by beating Dave Martin and John Spencer, Jimmy Chambers and Martin Clark and Dean Reynolds and John Parrott before Dennis Taylor and Cliff Thorburn stopped the youngsters' progress.

JOHN SMYTH

Born: 28 May 1928, Dublin, Republic of Ireland

Born in Dublin, John Smyth came to England when he was 21 and got a job as a train driver on the London underground. He kept that job for 28 years until he quit in 1978 to become snooker's first full-time referee. For a couple of years before that he had been calling himself a professional snooker referee.

Piccadilly Line champion
While on the underground John mostly worked on the Piccadilly Line and was six times the Piccadilly Line snooker champion. He has a top break of 72.

John started refereeing in 1967 and his first match involving a professional was between Jackie Rea and the amateur Sid Hood in the first round of the 1973 Norwich Union Open, which Hood won

4-0. He got the chance to officiate in his first World Professional Championship final in 1977 when he was in charge of the John Spencer–Cliff Thorburn match. Five years later he was the referee of the Alex Higgins–Ray Reardon match when Higgins won the title for the second time.

But one of John's most memorable moments was in the 1984 Benson & Hedges Masters when he had the privilege to be in charge when Kirk Stevens compiled his 147 against Jimmy White. John has, along with John Street, officiated at all Masters since their inauguration in 1975.

John has one son and two grandchildren. Sadly his wife died in 1972. In his spare time John loves watching westerns . . . he is an addict.

A former tube driver, John Smyth became the game's first professional referee in 1978. A year earlier he refereed the Crucible's first world final

JOHN SPENCER

Born: 18 September 1935, Radcliffe, Lancashire, England

Turned professional: 1968

First ranking points: 1974 World Professional Championship

There was no greater performance in the 1986-87 season than John Spencer's reaching the quarter-final of the Dulux British Open. One of the game's all-time greats, he had to suffer over the years as youngster after youngster climbed past him in the rankings. Furthermore, Spencer was afflicted with an eyesight disorder in 1984 which threatened to end his career completely.

He came to terms with his handicap but constantly needs to take medication. He concentrated on keeping his game together. And that determination was rewarded with the great run in the Dulux when he beat Tony Meo 5-1, Dave Martin 5-2 and Joe Johnson 5-3 to reach the quarter-final of a ranking tournament for the first time since the 1983 Jameson International. Against the 'Whirlwind', Jimmy

White, John pushed his younger opponent all the way but lost 5-3. Spencer led 2-1 at one time and pulled back from 3-2 to 3-all before losing. In making it 3-all Spencer showed some of the guile that made him one of the giants of the game.

Snooker . . . well, that's the name of the game

Trailing 74-16 with one red left, Spencer needed six 4-point snookers to win. He played brilliantly and picked up 23 points from

John Spencer holds aloft the World Championship Trophy after winning the first final at the Crucible

CAREER HIGHLIGHTS

1966
English Amateur Champion
World Amateur Championship
(runner-up)

1969-70
World Professional Champion

1975
Benson & Hedges Masters
Champion

1977
World Professional Champion

1978
Benson & Hedges Irish
Masters Champion

1979
Holsten Lager Champion

1980
Wilsons Classic Champion

1981
State Express World Team
Classic (member of winning
England team)

Rankings

Year	Ranking
1983	16
1984	13
1985	20
1986	34
1987	28
1988	27

five penalties by White. On the last, Spencer took a free ball, and cleared up with a 60, winning on the last black. In defeat John picked up the biggest cheque of his 20-year professional career when he banked £9,000.

The snooker career of John Spencer started in his native Lancashire when he was 15. Within a year of first picking up a cue he was capable of compiling a century break. Two years later he was called up for two years national service and gave up the game. It was not until 1963 that he decided to play seriously again. He entered the English Amateur Championship in 1963-64 and reached the final before losing to a man with whom he shared many great matches over the years, Ray Reardon.

Exhibitions at £14 a night!

Pat Houlihan beat John in the 1965 amateur final but in 1966 he got the victory he deserved when he beat Marcus Owen 11-5. John represented England in the World

In his prime John Spencer was one of the game's best long potters. Glimpses of the old Spencer were seen in the 1988 British Open when he beat Dennis Taylor 5-0 before losing 5-4 to Rex Williams

Championship in Karachi later in the year but was beaten in the final by Marcus' brother Gary.

In 1968 John, Reardon and Gary Owen all decided to turn professional and become the game's first new professionals since 1951, and like the other two, John enjoyed a successful career playing the holiday camp circuit and providing exhibitions for the paltry sum of £14 per night. That looks insignificant compared with the £5,000 Steve Davis costs today.

When the World Professional Championship was revived as a knock-out competition in 1969 the final was contested by two of the three new boys of snooker, Spencer and Owen, and Spencer avenged his world amateur defeat by winning the 73-frame final 37-24. Spencer could afford to enter only as a result of borrowing £100 from the bank to cover his expenses.

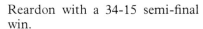

His World Championship rivalry with Ray Reardon

Since the return of the World Championship to a knock-out competition in 1969, John Spencer and Ray Reardon have met each other six times. This is how they have fared:

1970 (Apr)	Semi-final	Reardon won	37-33
1970 (Nov)	Semi-final	Spencer won	34-15
1973	Semi-final	Reardon won	23-22
1975	Quarter-final	Reardon won	19-17
1977	Quarter-final	Spencer won	13-6
1981	Second round	Reardon won	13-11

Reardon ousted Spencer at the semi-final stage in 1970 but when a second championship was held in Australia later that year John won his second title by beating the local man Warren Simpson 37-29 in the final, after gaining revenge over

The three-times world champion, John Spencer. His career nearly ended in 1984 when he was struck down with a serious eye disorder

Reardon with a 34-15 semi-final win.

Spencer and Reardon clashed in the first Benson & Hedges Masters final in 1975 and Spencer won that battle with a 9-8 win on a lightning fast table.

Three times 'Pot Black' champion

The television programme 'Pot Black' started the current snooker boom and Spencer won the title three times. He beat Reardon to win in 1970, Fred Davis the following year, and Dennis Taylor in 1976 to become the first man to win the title three times.

Spencer continued to dominate the battles with Reardon when he beat him in the quarter-final of the 1977 World Championship. John then beat John Pulman 18-16 in the semi-final before beating the Canadian Cliff Thorburn 25-21 in the final to become the first winner at the Crucible, and the first man to win the world title with a two-piece cue.

'The last time I got to a quarter final there were only eight men in the competition.'

John's comment after reaching the last eight of the 1987 Dulux

When the Guinness World Cup was held at Bournemouth in 1985, England's best known supporter, Ken Bailey, who lives in the town, was there dressed up in his John Bull outfit and carrying his Union Jack as usual. England had two teams in the competition and this led John to quip

'The guy with the flag won't know who to flag for!'

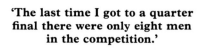

First televised 147 . . . well, it should have been

John won the Benson & Hedges Irish Masters in 1978 by beating new professional Doug Mountjoy in the final and the following year he beat Graham Miles 11-7 to win the Holsten Lager tournament at the Fulcrum Centre, Slough. But the tournament was even more memorable for John because he recorded the first maximum break in competitive play, although it was never ratified for record purposes. The event was being covered by Thames Television and should have beaten Steve Davis by three years to the first televised maximum. But it wasn't . . . due to industrial action the cameras were not rolling when Spencer made his magical 147 against Cliff Thorburn. Furthermore there was only a handful of spectators to witness the historic event.

John's only major win since the Holsten was in the 1980 Wilson's Classic at Manchester, when he beat Alex Higgins to take the £3,000 first prize. Those who saw John Spencer at his peak revel in his brilliant potting skills and cue-ball control and he was often compared with Joe Davis for the subtlety of his game.

John, who is now a good golfer as well as good snooker player, has enjoyed the financial rewards the game has brought him and in 1986 he opened his second snooker centre in Bolton. Sadly, the job took its toll on his 18-year marriage to Margot and they split up amicably in 1987.

Spencer (right) shares a joke with Canadian Cliff Thorburn before the start of the 1977 World Championship final. The joke was on Thorburn because Spencer ran out the 25–21 winner

Since his last World Championship win in 1977 John has never progressed further than two rounds in the event, and in 1987 it was a sad sight to see the first-round draw for the championship without the name of John Spencer in it. But the Dulux and the Tennents UK Open in 1986-87, when he beat Cliff Wilson and Kirk Stevens to reach the last 16, and his 5-0 win over Dennis Taylor in the 1988 British Open, suggests that John Spencer might be on his way back.

KIRK STEVENS

Born: 17 August 1958, Toronto, Canada

Turned professional: 1978

First ranking points: 1979 Embassy World Professional Championship

CAREER HIGHLIGHTS

1979, 1981, 1983
Canadian Professional Champion

1980
Embassy World Professional Championship (semi-final)

1982
World Cup (member of winning Canada team)

1984
Embassy World Professional Championship (semi-final)

1985
Dulux British Open (runner-up)

Rankings
1983	7
1984	4
1985	5
1986	9
1987	21
1988	37

In the three seasons between 1984 and 1987 Canada's Kirk Stevens had to endure the glare of publicity because of his admission to taking drugs. But worse, he has slipped from being one of snooker's 'golden boys' falling from fourth to outside the top 32 in the world rankings.

Born in Toronto, he started playing snooker at the age of ten and 'home' used to be the city's Golden Cue club. A professional since 1978, Kirk had, however, been playing money matches in Canada and North America since he was 15. Despite his age he looked only about 12 and when he offered to play older players for money his boyish looks lulled them into a false sense of security.

Shot out of town

Once, after hustling his way to winning $10,000, he was chased out of Dayton, Ohio, by a hail of bullets aimed at the car in which he was travelling. He never did go back to collect his cheque!

Kirk's parents split up when he was a youngster but he kept in touch with both of them. His father used to be a professional footballer with the Toronto Argonauts. When Kirk was 18 his mother was killed in an arson attack on her home. That tragedy was the motivation the brash youngster needed

Kirk Stevens on his way to his historic 147 break against Jimmy White in the 1984 Benson & Hedges Masters at Wembley

Kirk Stevens has enjoyed a prosperous time from snooker, as the sportscar shows. Sadly his life has been as traumatic as it has been successful. There is little the snooker world would like better than his return to form

'You have to take total responsibility for winning. It's never fate. It's always you.'

Some poignant and realistic comments from Stevens

to do something with his life and that is when he settled down to play serious snooker.

One of his idols was Cliff Thorburn and when Cliff gave an exhibition locally the young Stevens had the audacity to challenge him to a two-dollar match. Thorburn put the youngster in his place and when Stevens produced two of the filthiest dollar bills you could imagine, Thorburn still took them, hoping to teach the youngster a lesson.

Since then the two men have been friends and team-mates, although their paths have crossed several times on the snooker table. Kirk got his $2 back in 1979 when he beat Thorburn to win the Canadian professional title. Thorburn, however, has the slight edge in meetings since then and one of their best confrontations was in the World Championship quarter-final in 1983 which Thorburn won 13-12.

Great flair and individualism

It was in the World Championships of 1979 that the flamboyant Stevens was introduced to the British fans. Not only did he bring a great natural talent and flair to the championship but he also brought a touch of individuality with his white outfits and matching shoes. Despite reaching the competition proper at the Crucible, Stevens lost to the former champion Fred Davis in the first round.

The following year Stevens was a sensation. Emulating his feat in the 1978 World Amateur Championship in Malta when he became the youngest semi-finalist, he became the youngest person to reach the last four in the World Professional Championship. Alex Higgins ended the youngster's dreams of winning the title but in getting that far Stevens beat such notable players as Eddie Charlton, John Spencer and Graham Miles.

In his opening game, against Miles, and on the first day of the championships, he put together a 136 break with the black still to go. Had he potted it, it would have been a championship record. But nerves got to the 21-year-old and a pot that he would normally make easily was missed.

After that Stevens made rapid progress up the world rankings and was regarded as a tough competitor, but with a happy-go-lucky attitude. Despite rising to fourth, he had still not landed a major individual title, although he had been a member of the Canadian side that won the World Cup in 1982.

A real threat

The 1983-84 season saw Kirk arrive as a real threat to the top players. He reached the quarter-final of both the Professional Players' Tournament and Lada Classic, where Tony Meo ousted him each time. But after beating Steve Davis in the quarter-final of the Benson & Hedges Masters he was engaged in a great battle with Jimmy White in the semi-final. Although the Londoner won, Stevens savoured one of snooker's great moments when he compiled an official maximum break in less than 13 minutes.

'If ever I win that first title then everybody will be invited to the party.'

Kirk Stevens talking before the start of his new season in 1987-88

His confidence was sky high for that year's World Championship but it was White who ended his dreams in the semi-final with a 16-14 win. That defeat demoralised Stevens and he lost so much interest he virtually took five months away from the game. He played a lot of golf during his lay-off and got his handicap down to ten. Very run down, he spent a couple of months living with John and Avril Virgo.

So close to a title, then problems

He got his approach and attitude right and after beating Steve Davis 9-7 in the semi-final of the Dulux British Open he became the favourite to win that elusive first title when he lined up against South African Silvino Francisco. But it was Francisco who took the title by 12-9. Then there was more trouble for Kirk.

Francisco made allegations about Stevens being under the influence of an illegal stimulant. Investigations followed and Francisco was fined and had two ranking points deducted by the WPBSA for his outburst. Two weeks later his allegations proved well-founded when Kirk admitted in a tabloid newspaper that he had been addicted to cocaine since he was 19 and was spending something like $200 a day on the addiction. Happily that long drawn-out saga is now a thing of the past. Francisco has had his fine and ranking points reinstated but more important, in the summer of 1985, Kirk returned to Toronto to be successfully treated for his addiction.

However, a lack of personal management has seen him reach an all-time low in his playing career and a drop out of the top 16 ranking list. He is hoping his bad couple of years, on and off the snooker table, are behind him and just before the 1987 World Professional Championships he signed a

Stevens in his younger days: in 1984 he was as high as number four in the world rankings

The 'nearly man'

Kirk has reached only two major professional finals. He has, however, reached ten other semi-finals, but fallen at the last fence. This is his list of near-misses:

1980	Embassy World Championship	v Alex Higgins	13-16
1981	Yamaha International Masters	v David Taylor	3-5
1982	Jameson International	v Tony Knowles	3-9
1983	Lada Classic	v Bill Werbeniuk	2-5
1983	Winfield Masters	v Cliff Thorburn	2-5
1984	Benson & Hedges Masters	v Jimmy White	4-6
1984	Tolly Cobbold Classic	v Steve Davis	4-5
1984	Embassy World Championship	v Jimmy White	14-16
1984	Coral UK Championship	v Steve Davis	2-9
1986	Langs Scottish Masters	v Alex Higgins	2-6

five-year contract with manager Robert Winsor, who looked after Cliff Thorburn's affairs for a couple of years. Previously managed by Mike Watterson and the Golden Leisure Group, he is now installed as the resident profes-sional at the Winners Club, not far from his new Southgate home where he could well settle and rid himself of the feeling of homesick-ness that has afflicted him ever since he first came to join the snooker circuit in Britain.

Kirk Stevens (left) with Rick Parfitt of the Status Quo rock group

Stevens went into the most cru-cial season of his career in 1987-88 feeling relaxed and confident. A summer fishing with his father back home helped the relaxation process. And with the security of Winsor's experience behind him there is no reason why Kirk Stevens should not be hitting the headlines again, but for the right reasons once more.

'I just looked down my cue and all I could see were nightmares.'

Summing up his disastrous 1986-87 season

'I'm playing so badly I'm allowing for kicks!'

Stevens again talking about that dreadful 1986-87 season

'They helped put Humpty Dumpty together again'

Referring to the help John and Avril Virgo gave him during his troubled times

JOHN STREET

Born: 3 January 1932, Exmouth, Devon, England

The popular Devon-born referee John Street

Born in Devon, John Street was evacuated to the north-east during the Second World War and spent a couple of years in Bishop Auckland. After the hostilities, he contracted tuberculosis and spent 14 months in hospital. On his dis-charge he returned to playing his first love, table tennis, and was good enough to play in the English championships once.

Television debut

John married wife Jean in 1953 and they have three children and three grandchildren. A good League snooker player with a top break of 63, John started refereeing in 1960 and had his first professional en-gagement during the 1974 World Championships· at Belle Vue,

Manchester. His television debut was in the 1978 Benson & Hedges Masters. Both he and John Smyth have officiated in every Masters since it started in 1975. He took charge of his first major final in 1979 when he refereed the English Amateur final between Jimmy White and Dave Martin at Hel-ston, Cornwall.

After 18 years as an insurance agent with the Pearl Assurance John quit the job in 1986 to con-centrate to refereeing full time. He also acts as the president of the Exeter League and the Devon Bil-liards and Snooker Association. When his busy schedule permits John loves deep sea fishing off the Devon coast.

The first secretary of the Pro-fessional Referees' Association (founded in 1979) John has off-iciated in two World Champion-ship final: Cliff Thorburn versus Alex Higgins in 1980 and in Joe Johnson versus Steve Davis in 1986, when Johnson pulled off his exciting shock win.

DAVID TAYLOR

Born: 29 July 1943, Bowden, Cheshire, England

Turned professional: 1968

First ranking points: 1975 World Professional Championship

David Taylor was brought up in Manchester, a competitive snooker area that produced some quality players in the 1960s. David was no exception and when John Spencer won the English Amateur title in 1966 it was the spur David needed because he felt he was good enough also to win the title. And win it he did, just two years later. Furthermore, he went one better than Spencer and followed up his English success by taking the world crown . . . Spencer could only finish runner-up in the World Amateur Championship.

World champion
Taylor started playing snooker at the age of 14 and at 16 he was thrilled to be able to buy his own cue, and that was the start of his improvement. By the time he was 18 he was one of the best players in the Manchester area and his just reward came in 1968 when he beat Chris Ross 11-6 to win the English title. A few months later in Sydney, Australia, he beat local player Max Williams 8-7 to win the world title and in the process compiled the competition's highest break of 96.

That success prompted David to turn professional, but in the days when the World Championship was about the only event of note David struggled to make a living out of snooker until he got his chance to work the holiday camp circuit in the mid-1970s.

David worked hard and spent anything up to six hours a day practising. Roy Lomas, a good class player, spotted flaws in

The 'Silver Fox', David Taylor, playing his 'second' sport – golf, at which he is also a pretty useful performer

CAREER HIGHLIGHTS

1968
English Amateur Champion
World Amateur Champion

1978
Coral UK Championship
(runner-up)

1980
Embassy World Professional
Championship (semi-final)

1981
State Express World Team
Classic (member of winning
England team)
Yamaha Organs Trophy
(runner-up)

1982
Jameson International
(runner-up)

Rankings
Year	Ranking
1983	10
1984	16
1985	14
1986	21
1987	25
1988	28

The English and World amateur champion in 1968 David has not enjoyed the same success as a professional

David's game and he ironed out the faults. And in 1978 David enjoyed his best moment in ten years as a professional when he reached the final of the UK Championship at Preston after beating two of his old Manchester rivals, John Virgo and Alex Higgins, in the quarter- and semi-final stages. But in the final new professional Doug Mountjoy proved too good for David and ran out the 15-9 winner.

Snooker revival

Shortly after Christmas 1979 David enjoyed his best ever run in the World Professional Championship. He beat Fred Davis and then had a great 13-11 win over Ray Reardon in the quarter-final before he lost to Cliff Thorburn in the semi-final.

The following season saw David reach another final when he met Steve Davis in the Yamaha Organs Trophy but the newcomer from London prevented Taylor from winning his first title. Later that year (1981) David teamed up with Davis, and John Spencer, to lift the World Team title for England. At last Taylor had won something as a professional. In the early 1980s Taylor was ranked in the top ten and got as high as number seven in 1981.

David was still desperate for an individual title and in 1982 he met fellow Lancastrian Tony Knowles in the final of the Jameson International. Knowles was the new 'wonder boy' of snooker, but this was, perhaps, David's best chance of a title – after all, he had beaten Steve Davis 5-3 in the quarter-final, after Davis had twice led. But it was not to be and Knowles ended up the 9-6 winner.

Since then wins over Jimmy White in the 1983 Lada and John Parrott in the 1985 Tolly Cobbold English Professional Championship have been David's best results. He may well have done better in the 1985 Tolly Cobbold had it not been for his wife . . . David had started wearing glasses earlier in the season and shortly before his quarter-final match with Tony Knowles Janice stood on them. Knowles won 9-2.

David has slipped out of the top 16 and ended 1986-87 in 25th place in the rankings, and it was thanks to a great run in the Dulux British Open that his slide was not even greater. After beating the equally 'descending' Kirk Stevens in the last 16, when David was seen wearing contact lenses for the first time, he met another Canadian, Cliff Thorburn, in the quarter-final, but that was the end of the road for the Mancunian as Thorburn won 5-3 after Taylor had led 3-0. David is now ranked 28th in the world.

Not a bad painter . . .

Nicknamed the 'Silver Fox' because of his distinctive silver grey hair, David used to be a hairdresser in the days before he turned professional. He also worked as a swimming baths attendant and once had a spell picking vegetables in the Channel Islands. He loves Chinese and Indian food and when he gets the chance to sit down and relax at his Cheshire home he will either sit and listen to his favourite singers Barbara Streisand and Liza Minelli, or will be seen with paint brushes and palette in hand because David is a pretty useful artist.

Although David's individual record as a professional is sparse, he does however claim a world record for compiling three consecutive clearances with breaks of 130, 140 and 139 at Butlins, Minehead, in 1978. David is very popular at exhibition matches and for that reason will always make a living out of the game, but nothing would give him greater pleasure than to move back up those rankings, and in particular to lift that elusive first individual professional title.

DENNIS TAYLOR

Born: 19 January 1949, Coalisland, County Tyrone, Northern Ireland

Turned professional: 1972

First ranking points: 1975 World Professional Championship

When Dennis Taylor won the 1984 Rothmans Grand Prix at Reading's Hexagon Theatre there was not a fellow professional who was not pleased at his first major victory. A professional for 12 years, he had come so close, yet so far, on a lot of occasions and he must have been doubting his ability to win that first elusive major trophy.

He had beaten Alex Higgins to win the 1982 Irish professional title but that was only from a seven-man field. But his list of second places included 1975 and 1976 'Pot Black', the 1979 World Championship to Terry Griffith, the Tolly Cobbold Classic, Winfield Australian Masters and Wilsons Classic, all in 1980. He was roundly beaten 9-0 by Steve Davis in the 1981 Jameson final and it was Davis who again beat him in the final of the Tolly Cobbold Classic a year later. But since making the breakthrough in 1984 Taylor has improved remarkably, and is now a very difficult man to beat. His teaming up with Barry Hearn has taken his revitalisation further.

Played left-handed, just to get a game

Dennis started playing snooker at the age of nine and at 14 was as good as any senior player in his area. He was a regular player at Jim-Joe Gervin's snooker hall in Coalisland.

He came to England as a 17-

'Gottle of Geer' . . . stick to snooker Dennis, we can see your lips moving

'I've beaten Cliff Thorburn, the toughest player. I've beaten Steve Davis, the best player. But this year I'm the best in the world.'

Dennis after winning the 1985 World Championship

CAREER HIGHLIGHTS

1968
National Under-19 Billiards Champion

1971
National Breaks Champion

1982
Irish Professional Champion

1984
Rothmans Grand Prix Champion

1985
World Cup (member of winning All-Ireland team)
Embassy World Professional Champion
Irish Professional Champion
BCE Canadian Masters Champion
Kit Kat Break Champion

1986
World Cup (member of winning Ireland 'A' team)
Irish Professional Champion
Carlsberg Challenge Champion

1987
World Cup (member of winning Ireland 'A' team)
Benson & Hedges Masters Champion
Irish Professional Champion
Carling Champion

Rankings
1983	13
1984	11
1985	4
1986	3
1987	8
1988	10

The smile says it all: 'I'm champion of the world'. Dennis after his epic battle with Steve Davis in the 1985 championship which Taylor won on the final black.

'When something like this happens you realise that snooker comes a poor second to your family.'

Dennis talking after his mother's death

World number two, but still without a major title

Dennis was ranked number two in the world in 1979 and the following year he wrested the Irish professional title from Alex Higgins. He then made successful defences of the title, against Higgins and Patsy Fagan, before beating Higgins 16-13 in the first of the new-style knock-out events. But Dennis was desperate for his first win in a major tournament.

The following year Taylor caused quite a stir, not for his snooker play, but for his new 'Joe 90' spectacles which he unleashed on the unsuspecting public during the 1983 Benson & Hedges Irish Masters. The glasses had improved Dennis' play and they were largely responsible for his good run in the 1984 World Championship when he reached yet another semifinal, only to lose to Steve Davis, who beat him 16-9.

Everything was looking rosy for Taylor, one of the most popular men on the circuit, as he went into the 1984-85 season, but after beating Danny Fowler 5-0 in the first round of the Jameson Dennis got news that his mother had died suddenly and he withdrew from the competition. He is a great believer in the family unit, a belief instilled by his mother, and her loss was a great personal tragedy. The measure of respect she received was shown when 2,000 people attended her funeral in Coalisland. The closeness and warmth of his family persuaded Dennis to carry on playing and the next championship was the one he had been waiting for. He registered his first big win in the Rothmans Grand Prix.

In an emotional scene the whole nation shared Dennis' elation, and sadness, as he collected the trophy.

year-old and lived with relatives in Darwen, near Blackburn. He had not set his sights on a professional snooker career at that time, and he didn't even bring his cue with him. However, within two years he was the Under-19 Billiards Champion and he even won an international cap for England.

He turned professional in November 1972 and in his early days was earning a reputation for himself as a good and entertaining exhibition player, just as he is today. Taylor's first World Championship appearance was in 1973 but Cliff Thorburn, who was to

become one of Dennis' closest friends, beat him. Ironically, it was Thorburn who lost 10-2 to Taylor when he won the Rothmans event 11 years later.

The likable Irishman reached the semi-final of the World Championship in 1975 but Eddie Charlton beat him 19-12. Two years later in the first championship at the Crucible Dennis reached the last four again but Cliff Thorburn put the jinx on him once more. Another two years lapsed and Dennis made his third appearance in the semi-final. This time it was a case of third time lucky because he overcame fellow 'Lancastrian' John Virgo and set up a meeting with new professional Terry Griffiths. But it was the Welshman who came out on top and Dennis was 'bridesmaid'.

Alex Higgins and Dennis Taylor, Ireland's leading snooker players . . . or should that read 'leading golfers'?

Dennis Taylor with the Rothmans Trophy after beating Cliff Thorburn in the 1984 final. His win was one of the most popular, and emotional, in recent snooker

The greatest of all world finals

Since beating Thorburn to win at Reading, Dennis has not looked back. The greatest moment in his long and illustrious career came at the Crucible Theatre, Sheffield, on 28 April 1985 when he won the most titanic of battles to lift the Embassy world crown by beating Steve Davis on the final black in a last frame that took 68 minutes to complete. That victory took Taylor to a deserved fourth place in the rankings and immediately after the championship he teamed up with Steve Davis in the Barry Hearn Matchroom team. From then on Dennis has gone from strength to strength and has consolidated his position near the top of the rankings. He did however, suffer the fate of former champions John Spencer (in 1972), Terry Griffiths (1980) and Steve Davis (1982) by losing in the first round of the World Championship as defending champion, when Mike Hallett ousted him in 1986. But that is now well out of Dennis' system.

Dennis is very successful on the snooker table and one of the game's top earners. There was a time when that was not the case, but he has always had the one thing money cannot buy, the security of his wife Pat and their three children. Dennis is most certainly a believer in keeping that family unit together.

What a difference a world title makes . . .

In 1983-84, the year before he won the World Championship, Dennis Taylor was 14th on the money list with tournament winnings of £16,494 . . . this is how he has shaped up since then:

1983-84	£16,494	14th
1984-85	£150,876	2nd
1985-86	£124,802	4th
1986-87	£161,110	5th

CLIFF THORBURN, CM

Born: 16 January 1948, Victoria, British Columbia, Canada

Turned professional: 1973

First ranking points: 1975 World Professional Championship

Canada's Cliff Thorburn has remained one of snooker's most consistent performers since the mid-1970s and since 1976 has not figured outside the world top ten. No wonder his fellow players regard him as one of the hardest men on the circuit to beat.

Thorburn was the first great Canadian professional for more than 20 years. And it was after faring well against Rex Williams, John Spencer and Fred Davis, who toured Canada in 1971, that Cliff decided to turn professional.

A former pool player (and not bad at lacrosse either) Cliff won his first snooker championship, the Sidney Championship, when he was 16. His prize was a set of

'The grinder' lines up another shot

CAREER HIGHLIGHTS

1971-72
North American Champion

1974
Canadian Open Champion

1978-79
Canadian Open Champion

1980
Embassy World Professional Champion
Canadian Open Champion

1982
World Team Classic (member of winning Canada team)

1983
Benson & Hedges Masters Champion
Winfield Australian Masters Champion

1985
Benson & Hedges Masters Champion
Canadian Professional Champion
Langs Scottish Masters Champion
Goya Matchroom Trophy Champion

1986
Benson & Hedges Masters Champion
Canadian Professional Champion
Langs Scottish Masters Champion

Rankings

Year	Ranking
1983	3
1984	3
1985	2
1986	2
1987	4
1988	6

carving knives! Cliff's first professional match in England was against Dennis Taylor in the 1973 World Championship. The two men were later to become great friends; but on the day Cliff won their personal battle. In the next round he gave a great performance in narrowly losing 16-15 to Rex Williams. It was a brilliant start by a man unused to British tables.

First impact outside Canada

Thorburn at first made little impact on the professional game, other than in Canada where he had won the Canadian Open. But that all changed in the 1977 World Championship which was staged at the Crucible for the first time. He beat Rex Williams in the first round and had a great 13-12 win over Eddie Charlton in the quarter-final before beating Dennis Taylor

'Oh what a lovely feeling!' Cliff after beating Alex Higgins 18–16 in a great match to win the 1980 World Championship

again, to reach his first world final. There the former champion John Spencer was too good for Cliff as he ran out the 25-21 winner. But Thorburn had at last made an impact on snooker outside his native Canada.

During his quarter-final clash in the 1986 Embassy World Championship against Willie Thorne, Cliff's wife gave birth to their second son back home in Toronto in between the morning and evening session of the match. It is the first time a player has become a father while actually playing in a World Championship match

'Make sure you write about that after all the garbage that's been written about snooker lately.'

Cliff's request to the press making reference to Jimmy White's great piece of sportsmanship during the 1986 Benson & Hedges Masters when White called a foul on himself after it had been missed by the referee.

Three years later, however, Cliff was crowned world champion after he won a classic battle with Alex Higgins 18-16. Nearly 15 million television fans watched that final session as Thorburn ground down the Hurricane, and after the match it led to Higgins nicknaming Cliff the Grinder. That nickname has stuck ever since.

Cliff reached the semi-final of the Embassy in 1981 but lost 16-10 to Steve Davis. The following season he decided to move to England and play more tournaments. After losing to Jimmy White in the final of the Langs Scottish Masters it looked as though Cliff had made the right decision, but homesickness set in and he lost at the first hurdle in the next seven events, culminating in a first-round defeat by White at the Crucible. It was back to winning ways for Cliff in 1982-83 when he won the Benson & Hedges Masters for the first time and in the World Championship reached his third final before losing 18-6 to Steve Davis. But all Cliff's energy had been drained from him in his three matches before the final.

Three games take 17 hours
He beat Terry Griffiths and Kirk Stevens in games that both went their full distance of 25 frames and his semi-final win over Tony Knowles also went the full distance, of 31 frames. The last session in those three matches took more than 17 hours and the match with Griffiths finished at 3.41 am. Even though he didn't win the title, Cliff had the great honour of compiling the first maximum break in World Championship history during his match with Griffiths.

Cliff maintained his high ranking position in 1984 after losing to Davis in the final of the Jameson and in 1984-85 it was a series of near-misses for Cliff. He lost 10-2 to Dennis Taylor in the final of the Rothmans Grand Prix at Reading. Willie Thorne, like Taylor, won his first major championship at Thorburn's expense in the Mercantile Credit Classic and Alex Higgins dumped him in the semi-final of the Coral UK Open. The one win from a frustrating season was in the non-ranking Benson & Hedges Masters at Wembley. The season brought personal tragedy for Cliff when his manager Darryl McKerrow was killed while on a hunting expedition in Manitoba. But Cliff found help in the shape of millionaire Robert Winsor who was there to lend a hand and help Cliff out in his hour of need. His palatial north London home at Totteridge was Cliff's UK base and Winsor looked after Cliff's business affairs, and was soon negotiating lucrative off-the-table deals for him. In complete contrast to 1984-85 the following season was one of success, particularly in the first few tournaments.

Two great mates, Willie Thorne (left) and Cliff Thorburn shortly after Cliff compiled the fourth official maximum 147 break, against Terry Griffiths in the 1983 World Championship

A remarkable comeback

He went home to win the Canadian professional title in the summer by beating Robert Chaperon 6-4. Back in Britain he started off by beating Thorne 9-7 to win the Lang's Scottish Masters and then came from behind to beat Jimmy White 12-10 in the final of the Goya Matchroom Trophy at Stoke. White was leading 7-0 at the end of the first session and in the eighth frame was 74-0 up before Cliff won what was the turning point of the match. No frame in professional snooker had ever been won from such a deficit in a major championship. It set Thorburn on the road to a great victory.

White, however, had the chance for revenge in the final of the Mercantile Credit Classic later in the season, and took it with a 13-12 win. Thorburn and White did battle again in the Benson & Hedges Masters final and it was

---

In the 1985 Scottish Masters, Thorburn beat Silvino Francisco 6-0 in just 1½ hours . . . quick by Cliff's standards. It prompted him to quip to the press

'You can now call me the fastest of the slower players or the slowest of the faster players . . .'

Those remarkable long matches in the 1983 World Championship

Before reaching the final of the 1983 Embassy World Championship at the Crucible, Cliff was engaged in three matches that all went the full distance. The playing time of the final session of the three matches came to more than 17 hours. This is how they went:

Round	Opponent	Result	Length of final session	Finishing time
2	Terry Griffiths	won 13-12	6 hr 25 min	3.51 am
Q-F	Kirk Stevens	won 13-12	6 hr 11 min	2.12 am
S-F	Tony Knowles	won 16-15	4 hr 45 min	12.45 am

Cliff's turn to win, 9-5. Cliff ended a great season by reaching the semi-final of the Embassy where he lost to Steve Davis, but his season's earnings amounted to £192,000, second only to Davis.

Despite not winning a ranking event in 1986-87, Thorburn reached the final of the season's first tournament, the BCE International, but lost to Neal Foulds. He still collected over £100,000 from tournaments and finished fourth in the rankings. He is one of the toughest players to play against.

Cliff's wife Barbara could not settle when they first came to England in 1980 and she returned home. Cliff followed her and he then spent most of his time flying to England for each tournament

before Winsor made his home available. Cliff and Barbara have now bought their own house in north London and they and their two boys are settled.

In January 1988 Cliff, a Member of the Order of Canada (CM), left Robert Winsor to join Barry Hearn's Matchroom team. He encountered a setback in 1988 when he failed a drug test during the MIM Britannia British Open. He was fined £10,000, suspended from two ranking tournaments and two ranking points were deducted from him.

Cliff in action during the 1987 Fidelity International.

WILLIE THORNE

Born: 4 March 1954, Leicester, England

Turned professional: 1975

First ranking points: 1977 Embassy World Professional
Championship

When Willie Thorne beat Cliff Thorburn to win his first major professional tournament in 1985, it was no more than his due. He had been a professional for ten years and served the game well, but without the rewards he deserved.

As a youngster Willie showed outstanding talent and his successes in the junior championships in the early 1970s compared with those of Rex Williams 20 years earlier. Willie first started playing snooker while on holiday at Eastbourne at the age of 14. Upon his return he started playing on the tables at the Anstey Conservative Club, where Willie's dad was the steward. His parents then took over the Shoulder of Mutton pub at Braunstone in Leicester and fortunately for Willie there was a snooker table upstairs . . . and he had the luxury of playing whenever he wanted. However, he still chose to play at Osborne's, the local club, where he could get some good opposition.

Outstanding junior record

By the time he turned professional in 1975 Willie had won no fewer than six junior titles at both billiards and snooker, reached the final of the English Amateur Championship, where he lost to Sid Hood, and had been England's youngest international. But that fine record counted for nothing when he joined the professional game.

In his first seven years Willie's best performance was in beating Cliff Wilson 7-3 to win the 1980 Pontins Open. That same year the Thorne family had converted the former motor taxation office in

CAREER HIGHLIGHTS

1970
National Under-16 Billiards and Snooker Champion

1971-73
National Under-19 Billiards Champion

1984
Hofmeister World Doubles Championship (runner-up with Cliff Thorburn)

1985
Mercantile Credit Classic Champion

1986
Matchroom Trophy Champion

Rankings
1983	18
1984	12
1985	11
1986	7
1987	11
1988	13

During Granada television's recording of their documentary 'Who knows Paddy Browne?' they sent a TV camera along to cover Browne's match against Willie in the third round of the 1985 Coral UK championship at Preston. Willie was on a big break which stood at 127 with pink and black remaining when the film ran out! Willie turned round to the producer and asked

'Do you want me to hang on while you change the film?'

The producer was delighted. Willie duly sank the pink and black and was rewarded with a 140 break . . . the highest of the tournament

Willie is the champion break maker with over 70 maximum breaks in practice. He made one in the pre-televised stage of the Tennents UK Open in 1987, winning £6,750 – had it been in the televised stage it would have been worth £50,000. One of Willie's maximums was made while he had both legs in plaster following a go-kart accident in 1982

Willie Thorne with his first major professional title, the 1985 Mercantile Credit Classic

When he won the Mercantile Willie is reputed to have opened a can of 'Brasso' he bought when he first turned professional 10 years earlier in readiness for polishing that first trophy

An all-round sportsman as a youngster, Willie loved most sports but excelled at cricket and basketball. After winning the 1985 Mercantile he was asked what his ambition was now. The answer

'To appear on a "Question of Sport".'

When the BBC did eventually ask him . . . he couldn't make it!

Charles Street, Leicester, into the Willie Thorne Snooker Centre, one of the finest in the country. By the time the 1982 Embassy World Championship came around Willie had still to win a match at the Crucible in all his years of trying but then, after spending some time with David Taylor, it started to come good for the popular Thorne.

Taylor sorted Willie out mentally and at Sheffield his first Crucible victory came at the expense of Terry Griffiths. Another former Champion, John Spencer, was Willie's next victim but Alex Higgins was too good for Thorne in the quarter-final and the Irishman won 13-10. Willie had some consolation in that his break of 143 against Higgins was the highest of the Championship and the second highest in World Championship history after Doug Mountjoy's 145. But Thorne had at last shown his true potential, and he has never looked back since then and has shown a steady rise up the world rankings which culminated in 1984 when he made the top 16.

The Crucible 'success' was the spur Willie needed and the next season he beat Ray Reardon 5-0 to reach the quarter-final of the Jameson International, but Eddie Charlton inflicted a similar whitewash on Willie in the next round. He reached the semi-final of the Professional Players Tournament before losing to Tony Knowles and at the Crucible he enjoyed another first-round win, over John Virgo,

before Cliff Thorburn, who had become a great friend of Willie's, beat him in the second round.

Willie and Cliff teamed up for the Hofmeister World Doubles later in 1984 and they went all the way to the final before losing to the defending champions Davis and Meo. That was Willie's biggest success as a professional, but he still wanted a major individual title, and that came a year later.

1985 . . . what a year

He started the year by beating Thorburn 13-8 to win the Mercantile Credit Classic, and that was after a great 9-8 win over Steve Davis in the semi-final. His season virtually ended there so far as playing success was concerned. He was surprisingly beaten in the first round of the Embassy by Patsy Fagan. But in May he married Fiona, his girl friend of seven years. A few months later Willie became the proud father of twin boys Kieran and Tristan. He opened the second Willie Thorne Snooker Centre at Newmarket in 1985, and the choice of venue for the new club was quite appropriate because of Willie's love of gambling. A great friend of tic-tac man 'Racing Raymond' Winterton, Willie has the reputation for not resisting a gamble and would even have a flutter on the proverbial 'two flies up a wall'.

Teams up with Hearn

Willie enjoyed a good 1985-86 season but reclaimed the 'nearly-man' tag by reaching three finals and winning none. Steve Davis beat him 16-14 in the final of the Coral UK Open, Davis beat him again, 12-7, in the final of the Dulux, and in the Benson & Hedges Irish Masters Jimmy White beat him 9-5.

Barry Hearn signed Thorne as the fifth member of his team in 1986, and Willie started the 1986-87 season as number seven in the world. Apart from winning the non-ranking Hong Kong Masters and Matchroom Trophy (when he beat Davis) Willie slipped down the rankings slightly, to eleventh, in 1987. His best result was in reaching the Benson & Hedges Irish Masters final but he lost 9-1 to Davis, and his season ended on a losing note when he was beaten by Stephen Hendry in the first round of the World Championship at Sheffield.

The 'champion' break builder, Willie had 79 maximums to his credit, but none in tournament play . . . until the 1987 Tennents that is. In his fourth-round match with Tommy Murphy, Willie became the sixth man to register an officially recognised 147 break.

Willie on his wedding day in 1985 with guest Cliff Thorburn

JOHN VIRGO

Born: 3 April 1946, Rochdale, Lancashire, England

Turned professional: 1976

First ranking points: 1977 Embassy World Professional Championship

Since slipping out of the top 16 in 1984 John Virgo had to wait five years before getting back amongst the elite. But no matter what he does on the table, he will always make a comfortable living from the sport because of his great 'cabaret act'.

The 'Mike Yarwood of Snooker', John's impressions of his fellow players are much sought after for exhibitions around the country. His famous act was first seen on television when the BBC cameras had time to spare in the 1982 World Championship and they turned over to 'John Virgo . . . Opportunity Knocks' – and it certainly did. John got the idea for such an act, which he had started in his amateur days in Manchester, by watching Irishman Jackie Rea in exhibitions. In addition to doing his impressions John is also a very entertaining after-dinner speaker, and he is much sought after for that talent as well.

Oh, yes – he can play snooker as well

But we should not get carried away with his off-the-table activities. John Virgo is a very talented snooker player.

He was brought up in Rochdale, Lancashire, L. S. Lowry country, and his early snooker days were spent at Salford's Potters Club, a 'watering hole' for many of today's top professionals. Good enough to win the Under-16 title in 1962, John followed that with the Under-19 title three years later. He gained 15 England caps in six years and he ended his amateur career in 1976 by winning the National Pairs title with Paul Medati by beating another Manchester pair, Billy Kelly and Dennis Hughes, in the final.

> **'My husband is also a world-class snooker player.'**
>
> *This is normally Avril's retort when she takes a booking for John when people require him just for his comedy act*
>
> **'I used to go home and think how badly I played. Now I sit and watch other players all the time and realise they are as bad as me at times.'**

It would have been nice to leave the amateur game with the English title but Wirral's Roy Andrewartha beat John in the northern area final. Two days before losing to Andrewartha John compiled his first 147 break when his opponent was . . . Andrewartha!

Beaten by a toffee paper

A former clerk, John first showed his ability to compete at professional level when he reached the semi-final of the 1977 UK Championship at Blackpool before losing 9-8 to Patsy Fagan. Don't ever mention 'toffees' to John when talking about that match. A member of the audience opened a packet of toffees just as John was about to play a crucial shot and spoilt his concentration.

John reached the quarter-final of the same competition a year later when Preston had become its new venue and he rounded off that 1978-79 season by reaching the semi-final of the Embassy World Championship, his best result to date in the competition. He beat Willie Thorne, Cliff Thorburn and Bill Werbeniuk, all difficult men to beat, before meeting Dennis Taylor in the semi-final. But it was Taylor who went on to the final against Terry Griffiths.

Now, I wonder who John Virgo can be impersonating this time? Virgo's contribution to snooker goes further than his great cabaret act in which he impersonates his fellow professionals. He is the chairman of the WPBSA and, of course, it should not be forgotten what a good player he is

---

CAREER HIGHLIGHTS

1962
National Under-16 Champion

1965
National Under-19 Champion

1976
National Pairs Champion
(with Paul Medati)

1979
Embassy World Professional
Championship (semi-final)
Coral UK Champion

Rankings

Year	Ranking
1983	14
1984	18
1985	19
1986	19
1987	19
1988	15

In the 1979 UK Championship, an event John had come to enjoy, he achieved his best result as a professional when he won a great final against Terry Griffiths, the world champion, by 14 frames to 13. In the semi-final John had gained revenge over Dennis Taylor for his defeat in the World Championship by winning their match 9-4.

John seemed to be ready to launch an assault and build on that success but there was little to cheer again until the 1982 Jameson when

In 12 years as a professional John has just one major title to his name, the 1979 Coral UK Championship

he reached the semi-final but lost to fellow Mancunian David Taylor. It seemed to be coming good again for John, particularly after he reached the semi-final of the next event, the Professional Players Tournament at Redwood Lodge, but Jimmy White prevented any further advancement.

After losing in the first round of the World Championship to Cliff Thorburn in 1984 Virgo dropped out of the top 16. He reached the final of the Australian Masters that summer but lost 7-3 to Tony Knowles. He won the ill-fated Professional Snooker League which not only didn't carry any ranking points, but didn't carry any prize-

money either! It was not until the 1986 Dulux that John appeared in the semi-final of a ranking event for the first time since the 1982 Jameson. Willie Thorne beat him 9-4 but his three ranking points were good enough to consolidate his position in the rankings.

Steve Davis's 'bogey man' . . .

On his way to his first win in the 1979 Coral John beat Steve Davis 9-7 in the quarter-final. He didn't beat Davis again until the 1987 Dulux when Virgo won 5-4. It was the first time in Davis' professional career that he had failed to reach the televised stage of an event. John went on to the quarter-final where Davis' Matchroom team-mate Neal Foulds prevented John Virgo going any further.

John has moved away from the Manchester area and is based just outside Guildford in Surrey where he lives with wife Avril, always the life and soul of any party, and their beautiful baby daughter Brook who was born in 1987 and is very much the 'apple of daddy's eye'. The Virgo household warmly welcomed Kirk Stevens when he was having his problems in 1986 and they helped towards his overcoming them.

Virgo may look glum-faced when he is playing snooker but he has little to feel glum about. He is fully booked for engagements for a very long time to come. John and Avril, however, would swap some of those engagements for another win to go alongside his solitary major success back in 1979.

In 1987 John succeeded Rex Williams as chairman of the WPBSA.

In 1985 John bought a racehorse called Jokist. It duly obliged first time out

After winning the world title in 1986 one of the first people Joe Johnson went up to was Virgo, and the new champion asked

'How are you going to impersonate me, then?'

BILL WERBENIUK

Born: 14 January 1947, Winnipeg, Manitoba, Canada

Turned professional: 1973

First ranking points: 1974 World Professional Championship

CAREER HIGHLIGHTS

1973-76
North American Champion

1973
Canadian Professional Champion

1979
Coral UK Championship (semi-final)

1982
World Team Classic (member of winning Canada team)

1983
Lada Classic (runner-up)
Winfield Australian Masters (runner-up)

Rankings
1983	8
1984	14
1985	17
1986	24
1987	33
1988	47

By the end of the 1982-83 season Canada's Bill Werbeniuk had been a member of the Canadian team that beat England 4-2 to win the State Express World Team Classic and he had reached his first major final, the Lada Classic at Warrington. His success elevated him to number eight in the world rankings. Four years later he had not only slipped out of the top 16 but out of the next important grouping, the top 32, and was struggling in 33rd place.

Such a drop is a sad demise for a man who brought so much colour to the game. A great character, with his rotund frame he is the most recognisable of all snooker players.

Bill's first visit to England
Although born in Winnipeg he later moved to Vancouver, and first picked up a snooker cue at the age of nine. He turned professional in 1973 and celebrated with a notable double of Canadian and North American titles. He won the latter four times. British fans first got a glimpse of Bill's 20-stone frame in 1974 when he arrived for the World Championship. Between then and 1979 he came to Britain primarily for the Embassy, except in 1975 when he was invited to play in the Benson & Hedges Masters.

Bill made his first impact in the 1978 World Championship when he reached the quarter-final before losing to Ray Reardon but the following year Bill had a great win over the former Champion John Spencer, the number four seed, before losing, again at the quarter-final stage, to John Virgo. Against Spencer, however, Werbeniuk equalled Rex Williams' 14-year-old World Championship record when he compiled a break of 142.

After that Bill started appearing in more tournaments and established himself with a base in Worksop, where he could regularly be seen playing at the North Midland Snooker Centre.

A final at last
A third quarter-final appearance in the world championship came Bill's way in 1981 and it was Reardon who put him out once more, but this time less convincingly, 13-10. Reardon also thwarted Bill's hopes of making a major final in the 1982 Professional Players

After splitting his trousers during the 1980 World Cup Bill's captain Cliff Thorburn came out with such remarks as

'Well, it is a needle match.'

or

'I was hoping Bill was going to sew it up for us!'

Bill at the wheel of his mobile home. He has now bought a house and is not on the move anymore. Anyone want to buy a fully fitted bus?

Bill Werbeniuk has slipped outside the top 40 rankings from number eight in five seasons

'Bill represents all the world's heavyweights who long to be heroes but haven't got the figure for it.'

Janice Hale, assistant editor Snooker Scene

Tournament by knocking him out at quarter-final stage. But in his next tournament, the Lada Classic, Werbeniuk beat Alex Higgins, Doug Mountjoy and fellow Canadian Kirk Stevens before coming up against an in-form Steve Davis in the final. Davis won 9-5, but Bill had earned more recognition for his years of trying.

The year was far from over for Bill. During the summer he reached the final of the Winfield Australian Masters but lost 7-3 to Thorburn, who reaffirmed his superiority as Canada's number one, despite the challenge of Werbeniuk and Kirk Stevens.

A splitting problem

The three Canadians, however, have stuck together and represented their country in all World Cup competitions, winning the title in 1982 and finishing runner-up to Wales in 1980, and to Ireland in both 1986 and 1987. It was during Bill's match with England's David Taylor in the 1980 competition that he suffered one of the game's embarrassing moments when his trousers split . . . while he was on television! But little things like that don't bother Bill.

Bill gained further attention from the media in 1981 when the Inland Revenue allowed him to offset £2,000 of his income against tax to cover the cost of lager! Bill has suffered from a disease known as benign essential tremor since he was a baby, and his right arm

continually shakes. The only cure he found for it was to indulge in numerous pints of lager before and during a match. As it was for his business use, the Revenue granted the concession, which has since been withdrawn.

In 1982 Bill fitted out a 52-seater coach, in which he used to travel the country in preference to using hotels. It was fitted with two bedrooms, kitchen, bathroom, lounge and, of course, bar with draught lager. Bill has now bought a house in the Worksop area – so if you know anybody who wants a mobile hotel, let Bill know.

Sadly, Bill's game has deteriorated in recent years and in the 1986-87 season he won only one match, against Northern Ireland's Jack McLaughlin, the number 71 in the world. Bill's career plummeted to its lowest depths when he lost to Mark Bennett in the final qualifying round for the 1987 World Championship – it was the first time since 1977 that the jolly Werbeniuk was not present. Early signs in 1987–88 showed he could well have arrested that slide, as he collected points in the first two ranking tournaments of the season. He reached the Crucible stage of the World Championship but lost a closely contested match with Dennis Taylor by 10-8.

'Playing Bill is like playing for pints of blood.'

Cliff Thorburn during their 1986 World Championship match. Cliff won 10-5

BARRY WEST

Born: 24 October 1958, Wickersley, near Rotherham, Yorkshire, England

Turned professional: 1985

First ranking points: 1985 Coral UK Open

Having twice been unsuccessful with his application to become a professional, Barry West eventually took up his professional status in 1985 and immediately showed why he should have been accepted long before then.

In his third event, the Coral UK Open, he beat Eugene Hughes and Doug Mountjoy to reach the televised stage at Preston. On his TV debut he beat Scotland's Murdo McLeod 9-4 before setting up a meeting with Steve Davis in the quarter-final. The occasion and Davis got the better of Barry as the former world champion ran out a comfortable 9-1 winner. In the next tournament Barry reached the fourth round of the Mercantile Credit Classic before losing to Davis' stablemate Tony Meo.

Crucible debut

At the end of his first season West was ranked number 30 which meant he could miss a couple of qualifying rounds the following season, and when the Embassy World Professional Championship came around he had to win only one game before reaching the Crucible stage. He beat former champion John Spencer to register that important win, and it was another former champion, Ray Reardon, who provided Barry's opposition in the televised stage. The Welshman won 10-5.

Barry played at the North Midlands Snooker Centre in Worksop, a club that has bred many good players over the years, and in 1983 and 1984 he was a member of the all-conquering Yorkshire team that twice won the inter-counties title.

A second professional application was rejected in 1984, but happily Barry is now a member of the WPBSA, and in 1987 moved to a new base at the Doncaster Snooker Centre. The move obviously paid dividends. In the first ranking tournament of 1988, the Mercantile, Barry beat Willie Thorne and a couple of weeks later he had the best win of his career when he beat Jimmy White 6-2 in the English Professional Championship, before losing 9-6 to Neal Foulds in the semi-final. He lost to Doug Mountjoy in the World Championship 1st round.

Barry West showed in reaching the semi-final of the English Professional Championship at Ipswich in 1988 just what a polished player he is. Sadly there were no ranking points available

---

CAREER HIGHLIGHTS

1984
Pontins Autumn Open Champion

1985
Coral UK Championship (quarter-final)

1988
English Professional Championship (semi-final)

Rankings
1986   30
1987   29
1988   26

JIMMY WHITE

Born: 2 May 1962, Tooting, London, England

Turned professional: 1980

First ranking points: 1982 Embassy World Professional Championship

Jimmy White has been a professional only since 1980 yet he seems to have been part of the snooker scene for as long as most people can remember. Even more remarkably, by the time the 1988 World Championship came around White was only 26 years of age. He has packed so much, and won so much, in his time in the game, both as a top amateur and leading professional.

Jimmy White learned to play snooker the hard way, by chasing the next penny in money matches, not only in the London area, but all around the country, thanks to the help of his first 'manager', taxi-driver Bob Davis.

Robbo, the Matchroom minder/chauffeur, once said after touring with Jimmy

'After three weeks touring with Steve [Davis] I like to go home and have beans on toast. After three weeks touring with Jimmy I just want to go out and have a decent meal!'

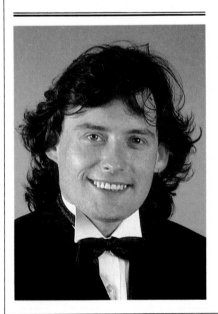

CAREER HIGHLIGHTS

1977
National Under-16 Champion

1979
English Amateur Champion

1980
World Amateur Champion
Indian Amateur Champion

1981
Langs Scottish Masters Champion
Northern Ireland Classic Champion

1984
Benson & Hedges Masters Champion
Carlsberg Challenge Champion

1985
Benson & Hedges Irish Masters Champion
Carlsberg Challenge Champion

1986
Mercantile Credit Classic Champion
Benson & Hedges Irish Masters Champion
Rothmans Grand Prix Champion

1987
Dulux British Open Champion

1988
Fersina World Cup
(member of winning England team)

Rankings

1983	11	1986	5
1984	7	1987	2
1985	7	1988	2

Jimmy White is the biggest earner in the game after Steve Davis

School, no; Zans, yes

White was brought up in Tooting and was educated at the Ernest Bevin Comprehensive school, where Tony Meo was a classmate. The word educated is used loosely because White didn't spend a lot of time at the school, most of his time being spent in the nearby Zans Billiard Hall. One day the headmaster, Mr Beattie, saw him play snooker and realised it was pointless trying to teach White anything else. All he needed to know was how to pot a snooker ball. Mr Beattie and White made a deal, however. White had to attend school in the mornings and the head would let him 'sag' school in the afternoon. It was certainly good foresight on Mr Beattie's part.

Bob Davis looked after both White and Meo but when they started winning big events they got too big for him to handle and Henry West, who managed Patsy Fagan at the time, took the two new charges under his wing.

White first attracted attention by beating Merseyside's Dave Bonney in the final of the Under-16 Championship in 1977. In 1979 he started setting records, the like of which had not been seen before, and have only been equalled since the arrival of Stephen Hendry. White became the youngest player to be selected for the London team in the Inter-Counties Championship and when he won the English amateur title at Helston in Cornwall he became, at 16 years 11 months, the youngest winner. In his 13-10 win over Dave Martin Jimmy compiled a 130 break which was not ratified as a championship record because of the generous pockets.

Jimmy went to Tasmania for the world amateur competition in 1980, and by beating Australian Ron Atkins in the final became the youngest winner of the title at 18 years 191 days. On the way home he stopped in India and won the national championship there.

Jimmy White with the Mercantile Credit Classic trophy in 1986

His 'whitewashes'

1982	Professional Players Tournament	Second round	Jim Wych	5-0
1984	Langs Scottish Masters	First round	Murdo McLeod	5-0
1984	Carlsberg Challenge	First round	Kirk Stevens	5-0
1985	Langs Scottish Masters	First round	Alex Higgins	5-0
1985	Rothmans Grand Prix (R)	Third round	Jack Fitzmaurice	5-0
1986	Benson & Hedges Irish Masters	Semi-final	Patsy Fagan	6-0
1986	Rothmans Grand Prix (R)	Third round	Tony Jones	5-0
1987	Mercantile Credit Classic (R)	Fourth round	Malcolm Bradley	5-0
1987	Dulux British Open (R)	Fifth round	Rex Williams	5-0
1987	Tennents UK Open (R)	Third round	John Dunning	9-0
1988	Benson & Hedges Masters	First round	Doug Mountjoy	5-0

This shot doesn't look all that easy, but Jimmy White will make it look as if it is

---

When Terry Smith, formerly of the Daily Mirror, *was once interviewing White, Jimmy said*

'I've put two inches on my cue.'

Smith asked inquisitively

'What does that mean?'

Jimmy's answer

'It's two inches longer . . .'

The 'whirlwind' arrives

On returning to England White turned professional and his presence was like a breath of fresh air into the game. Former world champion John Pulman described him as: 'The greatest natural talent that ever stepped into snooker'.

He reached the Crucible at the first attempt and put up a good show in losing to fellow-Londoner Steve Davis 10-8. In the first event of the next season, however, Jimmy continued his record-breaking sequence by becoming the youngest winner of a professional tournament when he beat Cliff Thorburn 9-4 to win the Langs Scottish Masters at the age of 19 years and 4 months. Jimmy immediately followed that win by beating Davis in the final of the Northern Ireland Classic. A new star was emerging.

Davis, however, brought him back down to earth with a 9-0 thrashing in the semi-final of the Coral UK Open and in the World Championship later in the season Jimmy agonisingly lost a great semi-final clash with Alex Higgins at the Crucible when the Irishman won 16-15.

Defeats by Ray Reardon in the final of both the 1982 Professional Players Tournament and 1983 Yamaha must have left Jimmy wondering whether he was ever going to

Jimmy White, with three ranking tournaments to his credit, has emerged in the last two seasons as the second most successful player in snooker, behind Steve Davis

result when he beat Thorburn in the final of the Mercantile Credit Classic 13-12. At last Jimmy had won his first ranking tournament, and in 1986-87 he did himself, his ranking position and his bank manager a big favour by winning both the Rothmans Grand Prix and Dulux British Open. A 13-12 defeat by Davis in the final of the Mercantile Credit Classic and a semi-final defeat (also by Davis) in the World Championship helped boost the kitty for the season and Jimmy's table winnings amounted to £225,000.

Jimmy has had a succession of managers since he turned professional. Henry West was his first manager when he joined the professional ranks in 1980. He then moved to the Manchester-based Sportsworld and when Geoff Lomas quit Sportsworld he took White and Kirk Stevens to the new Golden Leisure set-up. Howard Kruger acted as his agent for a while but in 1986 White completed Barry Hearn's magnificent seven after he bought himself out of his own contract with Noel Miller-Cheevers at Golden Leisure for £50,000.

A great joker, Jimmy loves winding up his fellow players. He also loves a game of cards. He can barely read or write but his large house at Wimbledon, which he shares with wife Maureen and two daughters, is proof enough that Mr Beattie and Jimmy got it right during his days at the Ernest Bevin Comprehensive school.

'I don't really know what his attitude is. I don't take a lot of notice of him.'

That was White talking about Barry Hearn in 1985. A few months later Hearn was White's manager

---

going to be the easy winner after leading 12-4 at the half-way stage. Jimmy pulled it back to 13-11, 16-15, and 17-16 before losing 16-18 in a great final. By now White was number seven in the rankings, yet surprisingly had never won a ranking tournament. That was still the case at the end of the 1984-85 season although Jimmy maintained his high ranking position.

The rise to number two

However, Jimmy moved up two places the following season after first reaching the final of the Goya Matchroom Trophy, where he lost a great final to Cliff Thorburn, and then by reversing that

recapture the form he showed in his early days as a professional, but he then beat Terry Griffiths to win the Benson & Hedges Masters and stop the rot. When he reached the final of the Embassy later in the season it looked as though Steve Davis was

---

'I'd like to be remembered as someone who won the game the hard way.'

Jimmy's own epitaph

JOHN WILLIAMS

Born: 8 June 1937, Wrexham, Denbighshire, Wales

What do John Williams' grandfather and former television newsreader Reginald Bosanquet have in common? The answer: bar billiards . . . John's grandfather was the British bar billiards champion in 1906 and for a while before his death Reggie was the president of the British Bar Billiards Association. It's a small world isn't it?

Well educated, John passed his 11-plus at the age of nine and when he left school, he had obtained seven O-levels. He got a job in the local steelworks and passed up the chance to become a professional footballer. An outstanding prospect at school, he was invited to join Bolton Wanderers as an amateur, but declined their offer because he worked on Saturday mornings.

After nearly 20 years in the steel industry he quit and joined the civil service as an executive officer in the Department of Employment and during that time he displayed his all-round sporting versatility by turning out regularly for the Wrexham civil service cricket team.

During the 1980 Coral UK final between Steve Davis and Alex Higgins John inadvertently picked up the white instead of respotting a colour. Showing the sign of a quality referee he turned to the players and said

'I'm sorry!'

and let play carry on . . . what else could he have done?

Rain stops play

John started snooker refereeing in the mid-1960s and he shot to fame when he was in charge of the famous 1973 match between Alex Higgins and Fred Davis at the Manchester Exhibition Hall when rain stopped play. Granada television sent a camera along to cover such an unusual happening and of course it brought John instant fame. He became the 'Pot Black' referee after Sydney Lee's retirement in 1981, having been the programme's marker for five years before being promoted to the 'middle', as they say in footballing terms.

Williams gave up his job in 1981 to become a full-time official and he is now the game's senior referee. Since 1974 he has been responsible for organising the Pontins Championships in his native North Wales. He has officiated in eight World Championship finals including the classic Taylor-Davis match of 1985. His first was the Ray Reardon versus Perrie Mans final in 1978.

John Williams, the game's senior referee. Born in Wrexham, John now lives near Shrewsbury. Had he not worked Saturday mornings John could well have become a professional footballer

REX WILLIAMS

Born: 20 July 1933, Stourbridge, Worcestershire, England

Turned professional: 1951

First ranking points: 1974 World Professional Snooker Championship

CAREER HIGHLIGHTS

1948-49
National Under-16 Billiards and Snooker Champion

1950
National Under-19 Billiards Champion

1951
English Amateur Snooker Champion
National Under-19 Billiards and Snooker Champion

1968-80
World Professional Billiards Champion

1979
United Kingdom Professional Billiards Champion

1981
United Kingdom Professional Billiards Champion

1982-83
World Professional Billiards Champion

Rankings
1983	30
1984	31
1985	27
1986	16
1987	12
1988	18

Rex Williams has been a billiards and snooker champion since the late 1940s but one of his finest achievements was in 1986 when, despite an abundance of fresh young snooker talent, he got into the top 16 of the rankings. Furthermore, the following season he improved on his position by climbing the rankings four more places to number 12. A tremendous feat for one of the game's senior players.

Williams first started winning in 1948 when he captured the Boys' Championship at both billiards and snooker at Burroughes Hall. He retained both titles a year later. Too old for the Under-16 Championship in 1950, he won the Under-19 Billiards title and the following year lifted both titles and beat current professional Cliff Wilson. He also won the coveted English amateur title and at 17 years of age was the youngest winner until Jimmy White in 1980.

Professional at 18

Williams turned professional at the age of 18 but it was at a time when both games were starting their decline and it was in the world of exhibition matches that Williams had to make his living.

In 1964 he was largely responsible for the re-introduction of the World Professional Snooker Championships, albeit as a challenge competition. There had been no championship since 1952, although a Professional Match-Play Championship had assumed the role of world championship between 1952-57.

Williams also played his part in reviving the defunct Professional Billiard Players Association, now the World Professional Billiards and Snooker Association, of which Williams has served as chairman. And in 1968 Williams was responsible for reviving the World Professional Billiards Championship which had been dormant for 17 years when he travelled to Australia to challenge the last holder of the title, Clark McConachy. Williams returned as the champion after a narrow victory and he successfully defended the title four times before losing to Fred Davis in 1980. The competition then reverted to a knock-out tournament and Rex has won the title twice, in 1982 and 1983.

Successful businessman

During the declining years of snooker Rex ran a successful cue-making business which he handed over to his brother Ken while Rex developed Rex Williams Leisure, the pool and snooker table business he set up in 1975.

On the snooker scene Rex twice

Rex Williams, the former Chairman of the WPBSA

round of the 1984 Coral UK Open that he attracted any attention from the media. But in 1985-86 Rex surprised a lot of people by picking up ten ranking points, including four for reaching the semi-final of the Mercantile Credit Classic. Jimmy White only just beat Rex 9-7 in the semi, but Williams had beaten Tony Knowles and Alex Higgins on his way to the last four. Suddenly the 52-year-old was enjoying a new lease of life.

'I feel 21 again.'

Rex's feelings after beating Steve Davis 5-1 in the 1986 Rothmans

unsuccessfully challenged John Pulman for the world snooker title at Burroughes Hall in 1964, and in South Africa in 1965. During his match with Pulman Rex created a world championship record break of 142 which stood until beaten by Doug Mountjoy in 1981. Shortly after losing to Pulman Williams played Mannie Francisco in an exhibition match at the Princes Hotel, Newlands, Cape Town, and became the second man after Joe Davis to compile an officially ratified 147 break.

Rex played his part in getting the world championship restored to a knock-out competition in 1969 and since then the best he has done in

Rex Williams and Fred Davis in younger days. They have 95 years of professional snooker between them!

the championship is to reach the semi-final, where he lost to John Spencer in 1969, to Alex Higgins in 1972 and to Graham Miles in 1974. His best chance of making the final was against Higgins when he led by six frames before losing 31-30.

As the number of ranking events started increasing in 1982 Rex found life among the ever-increasing number of professionals tough going and it was not until he beat Bill Werbeniuk 9-1 in the first

The Rex Williams story . . . part II

The improvement continued next season when he had a succession of amazing results in reaching the final of the Rothmans Grand Prix. He beat Mark Wildman 5-1, and then beat Alex Higgins by the same score. He completed a hat-trick of 5-1 wins by ousting Steve Davis and then beat the new 'golden boy' of snooker, Neal Foulds, 9-8 in the semi-final. Jimmy White spoilt the Williams celebrations once more with a 10-6 win in the final, but what a tournament it had been for Rex. That great run played its part in taking him four places up the rankings. And he collected £33,000 – the biggest pay-day of his 36-year professional career.

Rex's other involvement is with ITV as a summariser. He joined them in 1984 after transferring from the BBC.

As an administrator Rex did a lot for the game. As chairman of the WPBSA he had to tackle many sticky and difficult problems. Despite a vote of no confidence in 1987 Rex stayed on before resigning towards the end of the year after 13 years in the job.

His results on the snooker table in the last couple of seasons are ample evidence of his tenacity.

The third longest serving professional

Of the current playing members of the WPBSA, Rex Williams is the third longest serving professional.

1. Fred Davis	Turned professional	*1930*
2. Jack Rea		*1947*
3. REX WILLIAMS		*1951*
4. Eddie Charlton		*1960*
5. Ray Reardon		*1968*
John Spencer		
David Taylor		

(Perrie Mans turned professional in 1961 but he relinquished membership of the WPBSA in 1987.)

CLIFF WILSON

Born: 10 May 1934, Tredegar, Monmouthshire, Wales

Turned professional: 1979

First ranking points: 1982 Jameson International

Wilson is an outstanding potter, and can pot balls from virtually anywhere on the table. The snooker career of Cliff Wilson, however, has been in two parts. In the early 1950s his home town of Tredegar had two outstanding players, Wilson and Ray Reardon. When the two played each other you could guarantee a capacity crowd, and that would be for a normal league match.

The 'Alex Higgins' of the 1950s

The National Under-19 runner-up in 1951, Wilson won the title in the next two years and in 1956 won his first Welsh title, thus ending Reardon's run of six successive wins. While Reardon had the better record of the two men Wilson got great pleasure out of beating his rival in the semi-final of the 1954 English Amateur Championship, but he lost to Geoff Thompson in the final. Wilson's speedy style of play was typical of Alex Higgins', but Wilson applied it 20 years before Higgins.

Disillusioned with the game, Wilson stopped playing in 1957 and was out of the game 15 years. It was only when a friend asked him to help out when their club team was short that Wilson agreed to pick up his cue once more and immediately he got the snooker bug again. It was difficult to tell that he had been away, and within less than two years of coming out of retirement he was picked to play for Wales in the Home International series. And then, in 1977 he won his second Welsh amateur title . . . 21 years after his first!

World Amateur Champion

That win made Cliff eligible for the 1978 World Amateur Championship in Malta and he went on to

A great character, Cliff Wilson

win the title by beating Joe Johnson in the final. Cliff regained his Welsh crown in 1979 and shortly afterwards decided to try his hand at the professional game.

It was not until the 1982 Jameson International when he lost 5-4 to Tony Knowles in the quarter-final that Cliff showed anything like his true form from his amateur days. But away from competitive snooker Wilson was making a comfortable living from the world of exhibition matches, where he became one of the most popular entertainers. His ability to knock in big breaks and at the same time provide humorous banter is uncanny, and his exhibitions are a treat to watch.

Cliff Wilson is not only a good entertainer, but also a very good snooker player. Problems with his eyesight have been his biggest handicap in recent years but those problems now seem to be out of the way. In the 1986-87 season he collected nine ranking points, including quarter-final appearances

in the BCE International and Mercantile Credit Classic, and those performances helped him jump six places on the rankings to 17th. In 1988 he moved up a place to become one of the elite top 16.

The rivalry with Reardon has remained in the professional game and they have met each other four times. Reardon has won three meetings but Wilson won their semi-final clash in the 1984 Welsh Professional Championship. Cliff then lost to Doug Mountjoy in the final.

Audiences love to watch the extrovert Cliff, whose adventurous game makes no concession to safety play.

CAREER HIGHLIGHTS

1952-53
National Under-19 Champion

1956
Welsh Amateur Champion

1977
Welsh Amateur Champion

1978
World Amateur Champion

1979
Welsh Amateur Champion
National Pairs Champion
(with Steve Newbury)

1982
Jameson International
(quarter-final)

1985
Rothmans Grand Prix
(quarter-final)

1986
BCE International (quarter-final)

1987
Mercantile Credit Classic
(quarter-final)

Rankings

Year	Ranking
1983	20
1984	23
1985	22
1986	23
1987	17
1988	16

ROBERT WINSOR

Born: 10 August 1940, Padstow, Cornwall, England

Wealthy businessman Robert Winsor's hobby is birds . . . in the garden of his four-acre north London home he keeps flamingoes and storks, and he proudly boasts to being the only person in Britain to have bred a penguin in his back garden!

Robert Winsor is a self-made millionaire. When he was 18 he rented a shed for £1 per week and manufactured wire newspaper racks. That idea caught on rapidly and within no time large companies were asking him to design racking systems for their products and he became the biggest name in point-of-sale advertising.

Twenty-nine Rolls Royces

He owned the first of his 29 Rolls Royces when he was only 24, but prefers his top-of-the-range Mercedes these days.

A businessman from an early age, Robert was brought up in Cornwall where his father ran a grocer's shop. The family then bought a business in Surrey before they moved to a pub in Stoke Newington. It was there in the mid-1950s that Robert used an upstairs room as a disco . . . something unheard of in those days. He used to let the girls in for nothing and charge the lads a shilling each (5p) . . . he used to clear a few quid every Friday night. He was only 16 at the time but the businessman in him was coming through.

Robert's first sporting venture was into the world of professional women's golf, but being an excellent golfer himself (with a single-figure handicap) he soon realised he could beat them off scratch from the women's tees . . . he soon gave that up.

Golf brings Winsor and Thorburn together

His involvement in snooker was by accident. Cliff Thorburn was a friend of his and they had played golf together for a couple of years. Then in 1985 Cliff's manager Darryl McKerrow died in an accident and Robert offered to look after Thorburn's affairs. Robert maintains their friendship started when, after playing in a charity golf tournament at Finchley, he invited Cliff back for a cup of coffee and he stayed five years . . . Cliff has a different version of that story. He maintains it was in a four-ball at Wentworth. Cliff holed a 15-footer at the last hole which saved Winsor £20. Thorburn maintains that is the only reason they became friends. Golf is Robert's great love and in 1985 he was the founder of the Snooker Golf Society, which raises a lot of money for physically handicapped children. Robert has, so far, been involved with the supply of over 100 electric wheel chairs.

Cliff and Robert formed Robert Winsor International and subsequently took Jim Wych, Dene O'Kane, Paddy Browne, and Kirk Stevens under their wing. Everything Robert Winsor does is professional. The players in his charge could not be in better hands.

Sadly, the Winsor–Thorburn partnership came to an end in 1987 when Cliff joined Barry Hearn's Matchroom team in 1988.

'Do you like being a businessman or a snooker manager.'

That was the question a young schoolgirl put to Robert in a questionnaire for a project she was doing. She obviously believes you do not have to be a businessman to be a snooker manager

Robert Winsor managed Cliff Thorburn for two and a half years before Thorburn joined the Matchroom team in 1988

JON WRIGHT

Born: 10 August 1962, London, England

Turned professional: 1986

First ranking points: 1987 Mercantile Credit Classic

East Ender Jon Wright learned snooker the hard way, playing money matches, and with his *own* money. He was so keen to play his next match that he could not cash his Giro cheque quick enough to get the stake money . . . he was given the nickname 'Giro Jon'.

School took second place to Jon's love of snooker and when he left at 16 he settled down to playing snooker seriously at Hackney's New World club. Naturally talented, he has never had a lesson in his life but regards his father and Mick Faithfull as big influences on his career. His long potting is among the best to be seen.

Life has not been easy for Jon; he once spent nearly nine months living in a taxi! Because of the reputation that has followed him around, he was nicknamed 'The Wild Man of Bow'. But that aside, his snooker talents became apparent on the amateur circuit and

---

'My ambition this season was to get on television, and I could not have done it at a better time.'

Wright speaking before the World Championship meeting with Higgins at the Crucible Theatre

---

when he won the 1984 London title, a bright future was seen for Wright.

Well, it's one way of getting served in the bar!

He applied for professional status in February 1985 but was rejected. Later that year he was invited to compete in the World Amateur Championship at Blackpool as a replacement for Singapore's Eddie Loh. Wright was disciplined by the Billiards & Snooker Control Council for failing to turn up for two matches. He also hit the headlines at the championships for another reason . . . he attracted a barmaid's attention by standing in the middle of the room, naked from the waist down!

The B&SCC banned him from international competition for 12 months, but the ban had no effect because Jon had topped the new pro-ticket series in 1984-85 and was taking up professional status from September 1986 . . .

His first professional season produced some good results but he saved his best for the World Championship when, after beating Mark Wildman and Cliff Wilson, he qualified for the televised stage but lost 10-6 to Alex Higgins at the Crucible. Jon Wright has been hitting the snooker headlines for a long time. His snooker talent is good enough for him to start attracting attention for the right reasons.

CAREER HIGHLIGHT

1987
Embassy World Professional Championship (last 32)

Rankings
1987   53
1988   61

A new professional in 1986, Jon Wright brought a 'wild man' image with him

JIM WYCH

Born: 11 January 1955, Calgary, Alberta, Canada

Turned professional: 1980

First ranking points: 1980 Embassy World Professional Championship

In his first season as a professional and on his first visit as a pro to England Canadian Jim Wych reached the quarter-final of the World Championship after beating John Pulman and Dennis Taylor at the Crucible. It looked as though the decision to turn professional was fully justified even though Jim had forfeited the chance to represent Canada in the 1980 World Amateur Championship to join the professional ranks. At first he made little further impression, because he decided to spend most of his time back home in Canada. However, in the 1985-86 season he decided to concentrate on playing the circuit regularly and it paid dividends. He picked up three ranking points thanks to a great run in the Dulux British Open when he beat Dean Reynolds, Tony Knowles and John Parrott in successive rounds before being beaten by Steve Davis 5-2 in the quarter-finals.

All-round sportsman

A great competitor, Jim keenly plays other sports and is more than competent on the golf course. He is also quite useful at tennis and in his younger days was proficient at basketball and gymnastics.

Left-handed, he has a beautiful straight cue action and is a treat to watch. Jim teamed up with his fellow-Canadian Cliff Thorburn in Robert Winsor's stable in 1986. It was Thorburn who beat Jim in the final of 'Pot Black' in 1981 when Wych was the surprise finalist after beating Eddie Charlton, Alex Higgins and Ray Reardon.

After teaming up with Winsor, Jim had a poor season in 1986-87, despite reaching the final of the Canadian Professional Championship at the start of the season, only to lose 2-6 to his team-mate Thorburn. Thorburn also eliminated him in the first ranking tournament of the season, the BCE International, and fourth-round placings in the Rothmans and Tennents were as far as Jim got in the remainder of the season.

A win over Joe Johnson in the qualifying round of the Fidelity Unit Trusts International, the first ranking tournament of 1987-88, set Jim's hopes alive for a good season until Eugene Hughes beat him in the televised stage. Jim continued to show his ability by beating Stephen Hendry in the pre-televised stage of the Tennents UK championship.

CAREER HIGHLIGHTS

1979
Canadian Amateur Champion

1980
Embassy World Professional Championship (quarter-final)

1986
Dulux British Open (quarter-final)
Canadian Professional Championship (runner-up)

Rankings

Year	Ranking
1983	43
1984	41
1985	52
1986	32
1987	36
1988	38

Jim Wych looked about to break through in 1986 but has since hovered just outside the top 32